Kiln Theatre

CW00505095

By Suhaiymah Manzoor-Khan

CAST

Bilal
Usaamah Ibraheem Hussain

Hafsah
Humera Syed

CREATIVE TEAM

Writer
Suhaiymah Manzoor-Khan

Director
Sameena Hussain

Designer
Khadija Raza

Lighting Designer
Rajiv Pattani

Sound Designer
Helen Skiera

Movement Director
Natasha Harrison

Casting Director
Julia Horan CDG

Voice and Dialect Coach
Gurkiran Kaur

Costume Supervisor
Maariyah Sharjil

PRODUCTION TEAM

Production Manager
Marty Moore

Company Stage Manager
April Johnson

Deputy Stage Manager
Aiman Bandali

Assistant Stage Manager
Amara Bryan

Technician
Mae Elliott

Show Crew
Chioma Bayo

Wardrobe Manager
Keshini Ranasinghe

Revolve Programmer
Matt Neubauer

Lighting Programmer
Stevie Carty

Production Electrician
Paul Salmon

Production Sound Engineer
Dave Judd

Rigger
Jess Wilson

Production Carpenter
Taigh McCarthy

Set Built By
Kiln Theatre Workshops
Beam Studios
Revolving Stage Company

KILN THEATRE ARE GRATEFUL FOR THE SUPPORT OF THE FOLLOWING FOR THIS PRODUCTION:

Bertha Foundation
The Foyle Foundation
Royal Victoria Hall Foundation
Stanley Thomas Johnson Foundation

CAST

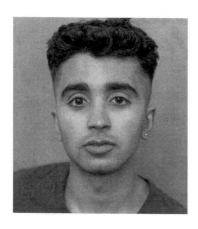

USAAMAH IBRAHEEM HUSSAIN
BILAL

Theatre credits include: *Brown Boys Swim* (Soho Theatre). His television work includes the upcoming BBC series *Virdee*.

HUMERA SYED
HAFSAH

Theatre credits include: *Great Expectations* (Royal Exchange Theatre); *FAITH* (RSC/Coventry City of Culture); *The Village* (Theatre Royal Stratford East); *The Arabian Knights* (Royal Lyceum Theatre) and *Anita and Me* (UK Tour). Her television work includes: *The Stranger* and *Hullraisers*.

CREATIVE TEAM

SUHAIYMAH MANZOOR-KHAN
WRITER

Suhaiymah Manzoor-Khan is an educator, writer and poet from Leeds. Her work disrupts narratives about history, race, knowledge and power – interrogating the root purpose of conversations about Muslims, migrants, gender and violence in particular. Suhaiymah works to provide herself and others with the tools to resist systemic oppression by unlearning what society and the education system have instilled in us. She was the runner-up of the Roundhouse National poetry slam 2017 with her viral poem, *This is Not a Humanising Poem* which gained 2 million views and was short-listed for the Outspoken Prize for Poetry in 2018. Suhaiymah is the author of poetry collection, *Postcolonial Banter* (Verve Poetry Press, 2019), co-author of the anthology, *A FLY GIRL'S GUIDE TO UNIVERSITY: Being a woman of colour at Cambridge and other institutions of power and elitism* (Verve Poetry Press, 2019) and hosts the Breaking Binaries podcast.

Her latest book, *Seeing for Ourselves: And Even Stranger Possibilities* was published with Hajar Press in 2023. This comes on the back of her book, *Tangled in Terror: Uprooting Islamophobia* published with Pluto Press in 2022.

Suhaiymah has written for *The Guardian*, *Independent*, *Al-Jazeera*, *gal-dem* and other national media outlets and her work has featured across radio and television, magazines and digital media. Her poetry, articles and books can be found on University and school syllabi. She has also been commissioned to write plays including: *Brown Women Do It Too* (Royal Court); *A Coin in Somebody Else's Pocket* (Theatre Uncut); *Whose Eyes Are These Anyway?* (The Albany); *My White Best Friend and other Letters Left Unsaid* (The

Bunker) and *The End of Diaspora* (Free Word Centre) and during her Writer in Residence at the Leeds Playhouse in 2021–22, her play *Take Care* had a public reading in Furnace Festival.

Peanut Butter & Blueberries is Suhaiymah's first full-length play.

SAMEENA HUSSAIN
DIRECTOR

Sameena Hussain is a freelance theatre director and facilitator based in West Yorkshire. Currently Associate Director at Leeds Playhouse, she's worked with Hull Truck Theatre, Opera North, Lawrence Batley Theatre, RSC and Soho Theatre.

Sameena's work is rooted in community and connection and since she started her career, she's been on a mission to remove barriers (both invisible and visible) preventing people from engaging with theatre and her projects have included everything from heritage projects and directing intergenerational performances, to creating and delivering artist development programmes and co-leading anti-racist strategies in institutions.

Sameena is passionate about making theatre a safe and brave space, enabling dialogue and connection.

Theatre credits include, as director: *Romeo & Juliet* (Leeds Conservatoire); *A Christmas Carol* (Hull Truck Theatre); *I Wanna Be Yours*, *Decades* (Leeds Playhouse); *La Voix Humaine* (Opera North/Leeds Playhouse) and *Our White Skoda Octavia* (Eastern Angles).

As Associate Director: *A Christmas Carol* and *Henry V* (Lawrence Batley Theatre).

As Assistant Director: *Dr Korczak's Example*, *Night Before Christmas*, *There Are No Beginnings*, *Europe*, *Road* and *A Christmas Carol* (Leeds Playhouse).

KHADIJA RAZA
DESIGNER

Recent theatre credits include: *The Secret Garden*, *Every Leaf a Hallelujah*, *Antigone* (Regent's Park Open Air Theatre); *Untitled F*ck M*ss S**gon Play* (Royal Exchange Theatre/Manchester International Festival/Headlong/Young Vic); *Sundown Kiki*, *The American Dream 2.0* (Young Vic); *Augmented* (Told By an Idiot/Royal Exchange Theatre); *Mixtape* (Royal Exchange Theatre); *The Flood* (Queen's Theatre, Hornchurch); *Talking About a Revolution* (The Barn); *Julius Caesar* (Shakespeare's Globe/UK Tour); *10 Nights* (Graeae/Tamasha Theatre/Bush Theatre); *Philoxenia*, *Hijabi Monologues* (Bush Theatre); *Bach & Sons* (Bridge Theatre); *Skin Hunger* (Dante or Die); *Funeral Flowers* (Roundhouse/UK Tour); *The Bee in Me* (Unicorn Theatre); *Great Ormond Street Hospital – Binaural Project* (Unicorn Theatre/Great Ormond Street Hospital); *A History of Water in the Middle East* (Royal Court); *Fly the Flag/Writing Wrongs* (Donmar Warehouse); *The White Best Friend (and Other Letters Left Unsaid)* (Bunker Theatre); *No One is Coming to Save You* (Bunker Theatre/Edinburgh Festival); *Cacophony* (Almeida Theatre/The Yard); *Loki and Cassie – A Love Story* (Almeida Theatre); *Spun* (Arcola Theatre) and *I Want you to Admire Me/But You Shouldn't* (Camden People's Theatre).

As Design Consultant: *Dugsi Dayz* (Side eYe Productions) and *Love Reign* (Young Vic).

As Associate Designer: *The Father and the Assassin* (National Theatre) and *The King of Hell's Palace* (Hampstead Theatre).

As Assistant Designer: *The Unknown Island* (Gate Theatre).

RAJIV PATTANI
LIGHTING DESIGNER

Trained at the London Academy of Music and Dramatic Art.

Theatre credits include: *Some Demon* (Arcola/Bristol Old Vic); *Hunger* (Arcola Theatre); *The Maladies, Testmatch, Yellowman, Statements After an Arrest Under the Immorality Act, OUTSIDE* (Orange Tree Theatre); *10 Nights* (Omnibus Theatre); *£1 Thursdays* (Finborough Theatre); *Trueman and the Arsonists* (Roundhouse Theatre); *High Times, Dirty Monsters* (National Tour); *Strategic Love Play* (Soho Theatre/Paines Plough Tour); *Hungry* (Soho Theatre/Paines Plough/Roundabout); *Sorry, You're Not a Winner* (Paines Plough Tour); *The Garden of Words* (Park Theatre); *Zoe's Peculiar Journey Through Time* (Southbank Centre/National Tour); *Hairy* (Polka Theatre); *The Flood* (Queen's Theatre Hornchurch); *SMOKE, Yellowfin* (Southwark Playhouse); *Alice in Wonderland* (Poltergeist Theatre Company/Brixton House); *Kabul Goes Pop! Music Television Afghanistan!* (Brixton House/National Tour); *Supernova* (Theatre503/National Tour); *Wolfie* (Theatre503); *The White Card* (Northern Stage/Leeds Playhouse/Birmingham Rep/Soho Theatre/HOME Manchester); *Mog the Forgetful Cat* (Royal & Derngate/National Tour); *Pilgrims* (Guildhall School of Music and Drama); *Winners* (Theatre on the Downs/Wardrobe Ensemble); *Final Farewell, Dawaat* (Tara Theatre); *Dirty Crusty* (Yard Theatre); *Dismantle This Room* (Jerwood Theatre Downstairs); *Nassim* (Bush Theatre/Edinburgh Traverse/International Tour); *Babylon Beyond Boarders, Leave Taking* and *Ramona Tells Jim* (Bush Theatre).

HELEN SKIERA
SOUND DESIGNER

Theatre credits include: *Mind Mangler: Member of the Tragic Circle* (Mischief/Apollo Theatre/UK Tour); *Museum of Infinite Realities* (Brussels, Technical Productions); *F**ked Up Bedtime Stories Series 2* (English Touring Theatre); *Cinderella, Red Riding Hood* (Theatre Royal Stratford East); *Not: Lady Chatterly's Lover* (Happy Idiot Productions/UK Tour); *The Long Song* (Chichester Festival Theatre); *A Christmas Carol* (Bristol Old Vic); *The Lovely Bones* (Birmingham REP/UK tour); *Out of Water* (Orange Tree); *Silence* (Mercury); *Here I Belong*

(Pentabus); *This Is Not For You* (Graeae GDIF/SIRF); *Instructions For Correct Assembly, Bodies* (Royal Court); *Imber: You Walk Through, Betrayal, The Magna Carta Plays* (Salisbury Playhouse); *The Encounter* (Complicité); *Good Dog, I Know All The Secrets in My World, Nhamo the Manyika Warrior, The Legend of Hamba* (Tiata Fahodzi); *House and Garden* (Watermill); *Harajuku Girls* (Finborough); *The Dog, The Night* and *The Knife* (Arcola).

As Associate sound Designer: *Viola's Room* (Punchdrunk); *The Dark is Rising* (BBC/Complicite audio drama); *East is East* (Birmingham REP/Chichester Festival Theatre); *Touching The Void* (Duke of York's); *Barbershop Chronicles* (National Theatre); *Cat on a Hot Tin Roof* (Young Vic/ Apollo Theatre); *Adler and Gibb* (Royal Court) and *I'd Rather Goya Robbed Me of My Sleep Than Some Other Arsehole* (The Gate).

As Operator: *King Charles III, Chimerica, Jersusalem* and *Enron.*

Other credits include: *Bussing Out* (MayProductions/UCL); *The Prick and The Sting* (Raucous); BLI-STA (Clean Break); *David's Bad Day, National Elf Service, Bad Altitude* (Fast Familiar) and *You Lay Your Hand Backwards* (Metta Theatre).

NATASHA HARRISON
MOVEMENT DIRECTOR

After studying at the Northern School of Contemporary Dance, Natasha went on to complete her Masters in Movement: Directing and Teaching, graduating from the Royal Central School of Speech and Drama.

Movement and choreography credits include: *When it Happens, Hir, Whodunnit (Unrehearsed), Whodunnit (Unrehearsed) 2, A Single Man, Building the Wall, La Cage aux Folles, Winner's Curse* (Park Theatre), *Good Enough Mums Club* (UK Tour); *Lord of the Flies* (Leeds Playhouse); *Linck & Mülhahn* (Hampstead Theatre); *Ride* (Leicester Curve/Southwark Playhouse); *The Bolds* (Unicorn Theatre); *A Game of Love and Chance and Hunger* (Arcola); *One Jewish Boy* (Trafalgar Studios); *Four*

Minutes Twelve Seconds (Co-Director & Movement Director, Oldham Coliseum); *A Christmas Carol* (Derby Theatre); *Mold Riots* (Theatr Clwyd); *Shakespeare Nation and Julius Caesar: First Encounters* (RSC); *Rocky Road* (Jermyn Street); *The Sweet Science of Bruising* (Wilton's Music Hall); *La Belle Helene* (Blackheath Halls); *Trouble in Tahiti & A Dinner Engagement* (RCM); *Handbagged* (Salisbury Playhouse); *Not Such Quiet Girls* (Leeds Playhouse/ Opera North); *Robin Hood and the Babes in the Wood* (CAST Doncaster); *Moll Flanders* (Mercury Theatre); *Wasted, Dear Brutus* and *The Cardinal* (Southwark Playhouse).

Other productions include: *The Rake's Progress* (British Youth Opera); *Blackthorn* (Paines Plough at Edinburgh Festival); *Tumulus* (Soho Theatre Studio/Vault Festival); *Tiny Dynamite* (Old Red Lion Theatre); *Ode to Leeds, Blackthorn* (Leeds Playhouse); *Twist* (Theatre Centre); *The Shed Crew* (Red Ladder); *Une Education Manque* and *Les Mamelles de Tiresias* (Royal College of Music).

JULIA HORAN CDG
CASTING DIRECTOR

For Kiln/Tricycle: *Two Strangers (Carry A Cake Across New York), The Wife of Willesden, Girl on an Altar, Pass Over, Red Velvet.*

Recent theatre credits include: *Oedipus* (Wyndham'sTheatre); *Kyoto* (RSC); *Player Kings, All About Eve* (Noel Coward Theatre); *Opening Night* (Gielgud Theatre); *King Lear, Romeo & Juliet, The Clinic, A Streetcar Named Desire, Macbeth, The Duchess of Malfi, The Doctor, Three Sisters, The Wild Duck, Machinal, The Writer, Summer & Smoke, The Treatment, Hamlet, Mary Stuart, Oil, Uncle Vanya, Medea, Oresteia, Game, Mr Burns* (Almeida Theatre); *School Girls; or the African Mean Girls Play, Tipping the Velvet* (Lyric Hammersmith); *Tambo & Bones* (Theatre Royal Stratford East); *A Little Life* (Harold Pinter Theatre/Savoy Theatre); *Sons of the Prophet* (Hampstead Theatre); *Blood Wedding, Jesus Hopped the A Train,*

Fun Home, The Inheritance, The Jungle, Yerma, A View from the Bridge (Young Vic); The Events (Actors Touring Company/ Young Vic); Cat on a Hot Tin Roof (Apollo Theatre); Appropriate (Donmar Warehouse); Harry Potter and the Cursed Child (Palace Theatre); Obsession, Hamlet (Barbican); City of Glass (59 Productions); Martyr (ATC); Hope, The Internet is Serious Business, Wolf from the Door, Adler & Gibb, Birdland, Khandan, The Mistress Contract, The Pass, Pigeons, Gastronauts, The Nether (Royal Court Theatre); Spring Awakening, The Seagull (Headlong); A Doll's House (Duke of York's Theatre/ BAM) and The Lighthouse Keeper (Birmingham Contemporary Music Group).

Recent television/film credits include: Together (BAFTA Winner Single Drama), Hamlet, Why It's Kicking Off Everywhere, The Exception, Departure and The Trial – A Murder in the Family.

GURKIRAN KAUR
VOICE AND DIALECT COACH

Gurkiran Kaur is a voice, accent and dialect coach from London and has coached over 50 productions. She believes in serving the people in the space ensuring inclusivity, equity and accessibility.

For Kiln Theatre: NW Trilogy

Theatre credits include: The Secret Garden (Regent's Park Open Air Theatre); Dugsi Dayz (Royal Court); Red Pitch (Soho Place/Bush Theatre); The Cord, A Playlist For The Revolution, Paradise Now, The P Word, Favour (Bush Theatre); Queens of Sheba (Soho Theatre); Sweat, Great Expectations (Royal Exchange Manchester); The Buddha of Suburbia, Falkland Sounds, The Empress (RSC);

Frankie Goes To Bollywood (Watford Palace); This Much I Know, Lotus Beauty (Hampstead Theatre); The Enormous Crocodile: The Musical (Leeds Playhouse), A Poem For Rabia (Tarragon Theatre Toronto); Brassic FM (Gate Theatre); I Wanna Be Yours (Melbourne Theatre Company); Wuthering Heights, Unexpected Twist (Royal & Derngate); Anansi The Spider, Marvin's Binoculars (Unicorn Theatre); I Wonder If..., Chasing Hares, Best of Enemies (Young Vic); A Dead Body in Taos (Fuel Theatre); Silence (Donmar Warehouse); The Best Exotic Marigold Hotel (Simon Friend Entertainment); Finding Home (Curve Leicester); The Climbers (Theatre by The Lake); Offside (Futures Theatre); Henry VIII (Shakespeare's Globe); How To Save The Planet When You're A Young Carer & Broke (Roundhouse); Extinct (Theatre Royal Stratford East); Good Karma Hospital (ITV/Tiger Aspect Productions) and Hotel Portofino (ITV/PBS/Eagle Eye).

MAARIYAH SHARJIL
COSTUME SUPERVISOR

Maariyah Sharjil is a designer.

She is a first-class graduate from BA Design for Performance at the Royal Central School of speech and Drama (2021). Before her design training, Maariyah worked at Sands Films as a costume constructor.

Her most recent productions include: Designer for Duck (Arcola); Costume researcher for Life of Pi (American Repertory Theatre); Design assistant for The Empress (RSC); Assistant Costume Designer for The Father and the Assassin (National Theatre) and Costume Designer for The Key Workers' Cycle (Almeida).

"Kiln Theatre has revitalised the cultural life of Brent and brings world-class theatre at an affordable price to people from all walks of life." **Zadie Smith**

Kiln Theatre sits in the heart of Kilburn in Brent, a unique and culturally diverse area of London where over 140 languages are spoken. We are a welcoming and proudly local venue, with an internationally acclaimed programme of world and UK premieres. Our work presents the world through a variety of lenses, amplifying unheard / ignored voices into the mainstream, exploring and examining the threads of human connection that cross race, culture and identity.

"This place was a special cocoon. Now she has grown and blossomed into a beautiful butterfly." **Sharon D Clarke**

We believe that theatre is for all and want everyone to feel welcome and entitled to call the Kiln their own. We are committed to nurturing the talent of young people and local communities, to provide a platform for their voices to be heard.

"I wanted to say thank you for creating the most diverse theatre I have been to. In terms of race, culture, class, age, everything – not only in the selection of shows and actors, but in the audience." **Audience member**

Kiln Theatre, 269 Kilburn High Road,
London, NW6 7JR
KilnTheatre.com | info@KilnTheatre.com
🅵 ⦿ 𝕏 ▶ ♪ @KilnTheatre

Supported by
ARTS COUNCIL ENGLAND

Registration No. 1396429.
Registered Charity No. 276892

CREATIVE ENGAGEMENT AT KILN THEATRE

From workshops to performances to events, we create free projects with and for people who live, learn or earn in Brent and North West London. Children, young people and adults from local communities are encouraged to have fun, be inspired, aspire, and have their voices heard through connection, skills building and theatre-making.

SCHOOLS

We believe all young people should have access to arts and culture and ensure our work is affordable and accessible to local schools. Our Schools Programme includes **Backstage Workshops**, **Teachers' workshops** and networks, **Resource Packs** and bespoke **School Residencies**.

YOUTH & PATHWAYS

The Youth & Pathways programme aims to develop the next generation of artists and audiences and create direct and transparent pathways into Kiln and out to the wider theatre ecology. Our **12–15 Youth Theatre** and **16–18 Young Company** support participants' development through devising and performing in multi-media productions. **Kiln Collaborators** receive paid training (at London Living Wage) in facilitation, leadership and theatre-making, and support the delivery and development of our Youth strand. We also deliver **Fullworks**, a week-long programme where young people learn from all departments at Kiln Theatre and attend a Creative Careers fair, which is open to young people across London, where they will hear from industry professionals.

MINDING THE GAP

Minding the Gap, our project for young people newly arrived in the UK, has been running for 18 years. We work with local schools and colleges' EAL and ESOL departments to provide creative drama- based sessions, which aim to develop students' creativity, confidence and engagement in the arts. Additionally, we deliver the **Minding the Gap Trainee programme**, through which former participants receive paid training (at London Living Wage) in facilitation and theatre-making and support the delivery of the programme. This year, we delivered our first **Minding the Gap Young Company** for previous participants who want to develop their performance and theatre-making skills further. We have also produced a Resource Pack and Teacher's CPD for EAL/ESOL teachers across London.

COMMUNITIES

The Communities work is rooted in Kilburn and Brent and celebrates the unique cultural and artistic life of our local area. Activity includes **Dementia-friendly Screenings**, and **Kiln Masterclasses**. This year we began delivery on **Celebrating Our Stories: the Kilburn High Road Project**, made possible with The National Lottery Heritage Fund with thanks to National Lottery Players. This three-year heritage focused project celebrates and platforms the hidden stories of the High Road and the residents, artists, businesses and organisations who call Kilburn home. Activity in Year One includes a **Minding the Gap Community Company** with newly arrived adults with experience of migration; **Chronicles of Kilburn**, heritage-inspired workshops in collaboration with local organisations, an oral history expert and artists; **Move at the Movies**, a movement based cinema programme working with adults referred through social prescribers; community co-curated **Town Hall Talks**, a full-day takeover of the building by local artists, organisations and residents; and **Listen Local Young Writers**, a project which supports 10 local young people aged 18–30 to write their first short plays inspired by their connection to Kilburn and research at Brent Museum and Archives.

For more information about our work and how to get involved, see our website **kilntheatre.com/ creative-engagement**, email us on **getinvolved@kilntheatre.com** or WhatsApp us on **07375 532006**.

SUPPORT OUR WORK

Kiln Theatre is a proudly local theatre with a world-class reputation. We create bold and engaging theatre which amplifies unheard voices. Our award-winning Creative Engagement programme offers free drama workshops, performances, and projects to local people, encouraging them to have fun and be heard.

We are committed to staging extraordinary theatre, inspiring the next generation of artists, and to keeping our ticket prices as low as possible.

Every year, we must fundraise close to £1 million to keep our doors open and our lights on. Will you help us?

YOU CAN SUPPORT KILN THEATRE BY:

- making a donation when booking a ticket
- making a regular donation each month
- joining the Kiln Circle
- making a major gift
- partnering with us through your company
- introducing us to your Trust or Foundation

KILN CIRCLE

The Kiln Circle is a philanthropic supporters' group that sits at the heart of our theatre. The Circle are given special opportunities to get close to the work on our stage and the artists involved in each of our productions. Donations start from £2,500 per year.

US TAXPAYERS

If you are a US taxpayer and wish to make a tax-effective donation to Kiln Theatre (registered charity number 276892), you can do so easily in dollars through CAF America. CAF America has full 501©(3) status, increasing the tax efficiency of your gift.

Scan the QR code, visit **Kilntheatre.com/give** or call our Fundraising Team on **020 7625 0132** to join our community of supporters today.

Registered with
FUNDRAISING **REGULATOR**   Registered Charity No. 276892

THANK YOU

We depend on donations of all sizes to ensure we can fulfil our mission to champion unheard voices and to make theatre for everyone. We would not be able to continue our work without the support of the following:

STATUTORY FUNDERS

Arts Council England
Brent Council Warm Spaces
Camden Council Culture Service
The National Lottery Heritage Fund

COMPANIES

The Agency (London) Ltd
Bloomberg Philanthropies
Investec
Nick Hern Books
Vogue World Fund

MAJOR DONORS AND KILN CIRCLE

Nick and Aleksandra Barnes
The Basden Family
Primrose and David Bell
Torrence Boone
Moyra McGarth Brown
Jules and Cheryl Burns
Mary and Jim Callaghan
Laure Zanchi Duvoisin
Dasha Epstein
Gary and Carol Fethke
Matthew Greenburgh and Helen Payne
Ros and Alan Haigh
Mary Clancy Hatch
Linda Keenan
Adam Kenwright
Jonathan Levy and Gabrielle Rifkind

Brian and Clare Linden
Frances Magee
Dame Susie Sainsbury
Jon and NoraLee Sedmak
Dr Miriam Stoppard
Jan and Michael Topham

INDIVIDUALS AND LEGACIES

Sue Fletcher
Nazima Kadir and Karl Gorz
Frances Lynn
Alison McLean and Michael Farthing
In memory of Harry Frank Rose
Ann and Peter Sprinz
Sarah and Joseph Zarfaty

TRUSTS AND FOUNDATIONS

29th May 1961 Charitable Trust
The Atkin Foundation
The Austin and Hope Pilkington Trust
Backstage Trust
Bertha Foundation
Boris Karloff Charitable Foundation
Chapman Charitable Trust
Christina Smith Foundation
City Bridge Foundation – London's biggest independent charity funder

Cockayne Grants for the Arts, a donor advised fund held at the London Community Foundation
John S Cohen Foundation
The D'Oyly Carte Charitable Trust
Esmée Fairbairn Foundation
The Foyle Foundation
Garfield Weston Foundation
Garrick Charitable Trust
The Hobson Charity
Jack Petchey Foundation
John Lyon's Charity
John Thaw Foundation
The Mackintosh Foundation
Marie-Louise von Motesiczky Charitable Trust
The Noël Coward Foundation
Pears Foundation
Richard Radcliffe Trust
The Roddick Foundation
Royal Victoria Hall Foundation
Stanley Thomas Johnson Foundation
Theatre Artists Pilot Programme
Three Monkies Trust
Vanderbilt Family Foundation
The Vandervell Foundation

And all those who wish to remain anonymous.

FOR KILN THEATRE

PEANUT BUTTER & BLUEBERRIES

Suhaiymah Manzoor-Khan

In the name of Allah, the Most Merciful,
the Most Compassionate.

All the praise is for Allah, Lord of all worlds of beings.

Oh Allah, send blessings and peace upon our master
Muhammad, his family, and companions.

Writer's Note

This is a love story.

Bilal and Hafsah are both practising Muslims. Islam is not
the topic of the play but one of its contexts. It is ubiquitous, a
texture, always present, therefore the characters must be played
by Muslim actors. Since their ethnic identities are key to their
connection, the actors should also be specifically Pakistani/
Kashmiri.

Both Bilal and Hafsah have unspoken religious boundaries in
terms of physical touch. They never touch. Instead, the intimacy
between them should be shown in the myriad of other ways it
exists. How intimate can a look be? What about a silence?
A touch held back?

The 'barrier' to their love is the impact of living in a society
built on brutalising capitalism, racial oppression, colonialism,
the traumas of historic erasure and the indignities of policing
and poverty.

Most scenes take place in London, things are often moving. The
play spans a year.

There should be direct engagement with the audience
throughout; eye contact and knowing looks with audience
members, possibly even during moments of dialogue between
the characters.

They know they are telling their own story, although we should
get the sense they are telling it separately, not together. It feels
as though it has already happened at times, and that it is still
unfolding at others, hence it is always real for one of them, even
as it is known already.

Choices must always be made, even if everything has already
been written.

Acknowledgements

In the name of Allah the Most Compassionate and Most Merciful. Alhamdulilah, all praise and thanks is to Allah who allowed me to write this play and granted me the wonderful team of people who facilitated its fruition. It is incumbent upon me to thank the people through whom God facilitated this project and they are many.

Thank you to my fierce and loving agent Davina Shah and to the always generous and caring Nafeesah Butt for first handing my poetry collection to Indhu Rubasingham who commissioned this play. Thank you, Indhu, for asking me the open-ended question of what story I would like to see that I had not seen before, and for trusting and believing that I could execute it. Thank you for committing to my story so whole-heartedly and ensuring we saw it through.

The journey of writing is never straightforward and the many drafts of this play were a result of kind encouragement, feedback and notes from a multitude of people who helped to pull out of this story the heart of what I wanted to uncover. Thank you to my ever-generous brother Zain Dada who has always made time for me, selflessly shared resources and knowledge and who has kept the path he paves illuminated for the rest of us, Allah bless you. Thanks also to maatin whose enthusiasm for sharing and listening informed the way I wanted to approach theatre in general and encouraged me to be firm in my vision. May Allah reward you also for all the ways you went above and beyond in supporting me through this process, you have taught me so much about what it means to follow the sunna of 'preferring others to yourself'. To Tom Wright who has been with the story from its inception, thank you for striking the perfect balance between trusting the characters and their world, whilst equipping me to bring them to life in brighter and bolder ways. Thanks for your generosity and humility, it has been deeply appreciated.

More thanks than I can express go to Sameena Hussain who not only directed this play's debut but introduced and made the world of theatre a possibility for me in the first place. Thank you for the very first time you asked me for a cup of tea in Leeds. Thank you for making me always feel so seen, for never gatekeeping, for listening and for pushing back. And thank you for fiercely loving the characters (and the North!) as much as I do, and committing to doing them justice.

I owe huge thanks to Amit Sharma and the entire staff at Kiln Theatre who facilitated this play coming to life for the first time – thank you for always being so warm and encouraging. A special thanks for being open to all the things I wanted to put in place to ensure this play wasn't just 'inclusive' of Muslim people in story, but also in reality – from prioritising prayer times and prayer space, to dry runs and more. Thanks for your willingness in these endeavours, I hope they outlast this play! To the entire production team, the marketing team and every staff member, thanks for your patience and efforts. Thank you also to all the actors who helped develop the piece and especially Usman Nawaz whose reading of Bilal made the play click for the first time.

Thank you to Humera Syed and Usaamah Ibraheem Hussain for bringing Hafsah and Bilal to life so lovingly for the first time. Thanks for caring and understanding, for sitting in the difficult places, and for working so incredibly hard. Thanks to the whole creative team who have first brough this play to life including Rajiv Pattani, Helen Skiera, Natasha Harrison, Julia Horan, Gurkiran Kaur, Marty Moore, Maariyah Sharjil, April Johnson, Amara Bryan and Joni Carter, you're amazing. A special thanks go to Aiman Bandali and Khadija Raza for going above and beyond your roles to inform and allow our Hafsah and Bilal to be as complicated as possible. To Khadija, thank you for designing such a wonderful first theatrical world for the play, giving permission for our stories to be abstract and symbolic rather than always open to voyeurs.

I must loop back to thank my agent Davina once more because her tireless commitment to having my back is one of the only things that saw me through this whole process. Thank you for ensuring we got through all the knots and challenges of this process in a way that meant the story and its intention were never compromised. That has meant the world to me.

And of course, this play would not exist without the constant love of my family to whom I will never do justice, no matter how many acknowledgements I write. Thank you for teaching me everything I know about dialogue, and especially about how much light and love can exist in a world of tribulations. And thank you for being the people with whom I learnt and continue to learn the most about character development and human complexity amidst love and for the sake of God. Allah bless you all always.

Thanks to my teachers who motivate me to try and always have lofty intentions. Whose transmission of knowledge that traces back to the Prophet Muhammed, may Allah's peace and blessings be upon him, inspires me to measure this play not by its reception in this world but by its benefit in view of the life to come. Thank you for teaching me to only deem significant what Allah deems significant and to not place false value on what does not deserve it. Allah elevate you.

Finally, thank you to my husband, Rizwan. Bilal and Hafsah would not be who they are without you, and nor would my understanding of love. Thank you for putting up with all the chaos of writing and putting on a play and for journeying through it with me. All praise is to Allah who made you the one with whom I share a soul.

May God forgive me my shortcomings in this project and protect it from being unbeneficial. Ameen.

My heart is at ease knowing that what was meant for me will never miss me, and that what misses me was never meant for me.

Imam Al-Shafi'ee

Characters

BILAL, *twenty-five, from Birmingham, has a beard and
    a proper Pakistani-Brum-boy accent*
HAFSAH, *twenty-three, from Bradford, wears hijab and loose
    clothing, she only has a very slight Yorkshire lilt*

Notes

A forward slash (/) denotes overlapping dialogue.

Text in **bold** denotes direct address.

*This text went to press before the end of rehearsals and so may
differ slightly from the play as performed.*

One Day (November)

In a seminar at SOAS University.

HAFSAH. You could tell from the start
  he was one of those Bilals that's let white people call him
  'Billy'
  it was the Docs
  I knew his type
  – wanted white approval
  no matter that it meant fetishisation from the white girls
  – probably a bonus if anything

  Complained about him to my friend, Hani
  we were all-too familiar with his kind from undergrad –
  no self-respect
  but instead of solidarity
  Hani of our nearing-mid-twenties said, 'Don't write him
  off'
  ugh
  Nowadays any boy with a beard and a bit of pigmentation
  is a potential in her eyes
  been trying to get me on Muzmatch for the last two years

  And now it's not just *her*
  Mythri, my new flatmate, got on my case before I'd even
  unpacked my bags
  said in Singapore all her Muslim friends date before
  marriage so why aren't I?

  Nice to meet you too, Mythri

  I've never seen a marriage that looks appealing
  rowing and arguing; limiting each other's dreams
  – thanks but no thanks

  Hani calls me a man-hater for that, but I say I'm a realist
  name one good thing men have ever done?

Exactly

**So I was ready to cancel this Bilal guy on sight, but
I couldn't, cos of his accent
full on Brummie
not white-washed, but proper pkstaani Brummie
you know what I mean – I'd do a take-off but I can't**

**Point is, it meant I didn't know *exactly* his kind, had to
give him some leeway
and now he's just finished a presentation based on his
year *living* in Kashmir...**

BILAL. Any questions?

HAFSAH *looks around for someone to ask a question,
nobody does.*

HAFSAH. **Oh go on then**
Not exactly a question
just wanted to thank you for sharing the testimonies
we don't usually hear from people on the ground, so, yeah,
it's appreciated

BILAL. Thanks for saying that
that's what's most important to me, too

**Honest truth?
I'd noticed her a fair bit by now
always cycled to seminar on this vintage blue Raleigh[1]
with a basket
I remember the first time I saw her, thinking, that's
haaard
you don't see that a lot, even in London**

**And there was the time we had to watch this old
Bollywood movie in class
– she was the only other person who needed subtitles
I was relieved I weren't alone, but she was embarrassed
the bleeding Italian students didn't need them and we
flipping did**

---

1. Raleigh said as 'Rally', a bicycle brand.

**She's the studious type though, so I could see why it
annoyed her
tried giving her a sympathetic look but she just looked
away
not sure what that's about – ain't like she's shy
– talks a mile a minute when it comes to colonialism**

HAFSAH. **Seminar ends and I head out
give him a nod, and as I do**

BILAL. Salaams,
thanks for what you said about the testimonies by the way,
took ages to collect

HAFSAH. No worries, well done

She continues to leave.

BILAL. D'ya – think I've seen you on a bike haven't I?
Blue Raleigh with the basket?

HAFSAH….Do you need my proof of license?

BILAL. I clocked it cos it's a nice bike

HAFSAH. Trying to do London on a budget so

BILAL. Not lived here long?

HAFSAH. Month and a bit

BILAL. Where ya from then? I can't tell from your ac/cent

HAFSAH. / Bradford

BILAL. Achhaa?

HAFSAH. Yeah, I know I've lost my 'ey-up' edge but
if you'd heard me when I was five you'd believe me

BILAL. Bradford Pakstaani? Here in SOAS?
That's made my day!
You lot are haaard
Chasing the National Front out the city? Them riots back in
day?
Bradford zindabad!

HAFSAH. I'll take that!
  Usually menace of the nation aren't we?
  – second only to you lot

BILAL. What you doing all the way in London then?
  Masters?

HAFSAH. Gender Studies

BILAL. Gender Studies?
  Zabardast!

HAFSAH. You're undergrad right?

BILAL. South Asia Studies
  Bane of my bleeding life

HAFSAH. That bad?

BILAL. Don't get me started

HAFSAH. Surely it'll help with not needing subtitles soon?

BILAL. I'm not even interested in Hindi or Urdu
  my heart's in Pahari

HAFSAH. Mirpuri?

BILAL. I prefer calling it Pahari, 'Mirpuri' feels loaded
  sometimes

HAFSAH. Oh right, do they teach that here?

BILAL. I wish!
  Barely recognised anywhere even though half us so-called
  'Pakistanis' speak it

  I just wanna understand the poetry, the spiritual sirrs[2] my
  Nani says casually

HAFSAH. Same issue here
  my grandparents have this specific Punjabi dialect I can't
  'learn' anywhere
  I understand a lot – but when I open my mouth it's just

BILAL. I get ya

---

2. 'Secrets' in Arabic

HAFSAH. Still better than my sisters though

BILAL. Younger?

HAFSAH. Course

BILAL. I'm youngest too that's why I'm worst

Whereabouts in the Punjab you lot from?

HAFSAH. Near Jhelum

BILAL. You know what's-his-name? Fanon?
Have you read his erm /

HAFSAH. / *Black Skin; White Masks*?

BILAL. No, *The Wretched of the Earth*?

HAFSAH. **Come on, it's SOAS**

BILAL. When *I* read it, I remember thinking, *what are we then*?
and I mean 'we' very specifically by the way

'South Asian' don't mean anything
What have I got in common with someone in, I don't know,
California
with roots in South India?

HAFSAH. Essentialising and Eurocentric, I get you /

BILAL. / Exactly! Essentialising and Eurocentric – that's it!
So I was thinking what are *we*?
The – not even Pakistani – forget that *essentialising* flipping
construct
I'm not talking Lahore, Karachi, let alone poor Balochistan
or Sindh

I mean the Pahari, Pothwari – even you Northern Punjabis
that diaspora in Britain specifically – what are *we*?

D'ya know about the Pothwari-plateau?

HAFSAH. Little bit

BILAL *uses his hands to draw out as he describes it.*

BILAL. It's this flat stretch of land right
from Jhelum on this side, to the Indus River on the other
the north of the Punjab – your lot – up to our ends, Mirpur,
Kashmir
top-right corner of Pakistan

HAFSAH. It's where most 'Pakistanis' in Bradford and Brum
are from
I did some work / on this actually

BILAL. / This is what I'm saying man!
We're from that *specific* square of land
and land shapes everything – the work ya do, food ya eat,
dialect ya speak
that's the *we* I'm talking about

HAFSAH. Right... and Fanon?

BILAL. D'ya know the word *becharay*? What it means?

HAFSAH. 'Poor thing'?
Like, when you pity someone?

BILAL. What d'ya think of this: *dunya ke becharay*

HAFSAH. The... world's... pitiful?

Is that meant to be 'wretched of the earth'?

BILAL *is vindicated*.

BILAL. That's it, that's us man: becharay

HAFSAH *is troubled*.

HAFSAH. Not sure how Fanon would feel about that... but,
okay

Gentle pause.

I've got to get / off to another

BILAL. / D'ya like tea?

HAFSAH. Bit more of a hot-chocolate person to be honest

BILAL. How 'bout ya take my number
and if ya wanna continue this convo over a hot choc some
time, holla at me?

HAFSAH. **Er**
　　Okay, I guess
　　Do you wanna put it in?

　　As BILAL *taps his number into her phone.*

　　Can I ask you something, Bilal?

BILAL. Anything

HAFSAH. Okay but be honest
　　Have you ever let white people call you 'Billy'?

BILAL. **Rah**
　　That's a dark question man, sure you want the answer?

HAFSAH. Think I just got it

　　He laughs, she is unimpressed.

　　Asalaamualaykum Bilal

BILAL. Walaykum-asalaam Hafsah from Bradford Sharif

One and a Half Months (January)

On campus, lunch break.

BILAL. **We've just left the weekly seminar**
　　sitting in the park in a way that's become a little routine
　　me with my coffee, her with her hot choccy

　　She never did text me ya know
　　but I got her the drinkable choc in advance of the next
　　seminar
　　reckon she was a bit impressed cos she sat with me for
　　a while afterwards

　　But then she *still* **didn't text me**
　　so the week after I actually did the reading for class just
　　so I could ask her about it

it was interesting as well ya know – 1980s Pakistan was
on a mad one yaara

Still no text, but the next week she lent me Ambedkar's
Annhiliation of Caste
that's a *heavy* book bro
sat in the park for a full half-hour, her telling me 'bout it
can't say I flipping followed but I got gassed about
annihilating caste still

A month later and I *still* don't have the girl's flipping
number
but here we are in a cheeky little groove

So don't say chivalry's dead yeah, Billy's got its back
– shi–, I mean Bilal

She's holding out another book now, ya Rabb![3]

HAFSAH. Seen this?

BILAL. Alhambra Palace?

HAFSAH. Yeah, in Granada

Hani said a guy only ever gives a girl his number for one
reason

I told her it's not like that – it's more a subject-based
connection – intellectual
and besides, you don't find people from places like
Bradford and Birmingham here
we see things in a similar way – see the flaws of academia
more clearly, that's all

I didn't text him though, just in case
even though he waits for me at the door every week
don't want him getting the wrong idea

Mythri's been on my back about making sure he's pious
enough
pious enough for what?? S*he's* not even Muslim!
– comes into the kitchen one day announcing:

---

3. 'Oh God.'

'good news is, we know he prays,
I saw him going into the prayer room every prayer time
today'

I told her, even if I was going to consider marrying
someone in the *distant future*
I'd care more about his character
anyone can pray five times a day, but Islam is *who you are*
how you treat your mum
how you speak to kids
that kind of stuff
you can't run a shady spy operation on that

She said, 'maybe not, but you can test it'
How? Am I some sort of gameshow host?

She shakes her head.

BILAL. What class is this this for?

HAFSAH. Just took it out for research – for my novella
   you ever been?

BILAL. I've never even been to Spain
   I thought your novel was sci-fi?

HAFSAH. Novel*la*
   It is – I just wanted some architectural inspiration for my
   world

   I got to go on once you know – Alhambra
   the tour guide showed us how the architects had engraved
   even into tiny leaves in the wall things like 'laa ilaha ill-
   Allah'[4]
   or God's names

   I thought, even if I start working on the novel of my dreams
   right here right now
   it'll never be so carefully thought through
   so intentionally a form of worship

BILAL. **Hers probably would be**

---

4. There is no deity except Allah.

Makes ya think, don't it?
These architects using their tools to glorify God
Then there's us – well me – studying a flipping area-studies
degree!

HAFSAH. What do you mean?

BILAL. **She takes the book back**

I mean I started this cos of language right – Pahari and Urdu
at first, then Arabic, Farsi – they're all connected
but I get stuck on the form, you get me? Vocab, grammar
That's not what they were using the language *for*
Like them – they were using those buildings for *GOD*
we get stuck thinking worship is just praying, fasting, rituals
not the actual purpose of our lives

HAFSAH *looks to audience with raised eyebrows.*

HAFSAH. Go on?

BILAL. Imagine if we were intentional?
Like, 'I'm gonna go to class to learn language to unlock the
Quran'
or, 'I'm gonna drink this coffee to energise myself so I'm
more present in my prayer'
or, 'I'm gonna chat to Hafsah cos her conversations stimulate
my mind' ya get me?

HAFSAH *looks away sharply and tries not to blush, chuckles
a little.*

We've got a long flipping way to go haven't we?

Beat.

HAFSAH. I always think of that Hadith Qudsi[5] my mum quotes,
where Allah says, 'I am as my servant expects me to be'
– if you think of Allah as harsh and judgemental, He is
but if you think of Him as unconditionally merciful, He will
be

I mean I should actually study, obviously, but in essence:
Think good of God, that's how I see it

5. A special category of narrations which are attributed to God.

BILAL. **I always remember her saying that**
it was the first time – dunno
something about her sitting on that bench in Russell
Square
that turquoise blue she always wore
telling me we could live like that, real Muslimeen

Beat.

Did I tell ya I was studying Accountancy before?

HAFSAH. Accountancy? You?

BILAL. I know, I know
My mate Abdulla used to say – 'bro you'd make a sick
accountant in Dadyal, but not sure about Dudley'

Know what though?
I'm starting to think accountancy – that's what men like me
should stick to

HAFSAH. 'Men like you'?

BILAL. Meray tarhan kay aadmay[6]

HAFSAH. Achhaa
Teray jesay banday?[7]

They laugh.

BILAL. Mum works two jobs right? Always has
and Dad's been a taxi driver most of his life
that's forty years Hafsah, do you know what that's like?
with accountancy I could have actually *contributed*

HAFSAH. My grandad and my dad were both driving
instructors
well, I guess my dad still is

BILAL. Unsure?

HAFSAH. Don't see him much

BILAL. There ya go

6. 'Men like me' in Urdu.
7. 'Men like you' in Punjabi.

HAFSAH. What?

BILAL. Single mothers across this whole becharay diaspora
Even when the dads are there they're not

They go quiet for a moment.

Mine also pissed off – years ago
left Mum with a mortgage she'll never finish paying off
and when she got married again *that* p–[8] just left her with an
extra mouth to feed – never sent a penny in maintenance
I saw him once, coming out a flipping Betfred! MashaAllah
uncle ji!

Pause.

Forget that anyway, ya hungry?

HAFSAH. **He takes a tupperware out of his bag**
a sandwich, handmade
opens it up and splits it, passes me the bigger half

What's in this?

BILAL. You tell me – no ya can't look

HAFSAH. Okay okay fine, bismillah

HAFSAH *bites into it hesitantly.*

Peanut butter?

BILAL. That's part one

HAFSAH. And something sweet, not –
hmm, squidgy…
I'm not sure?

BILAL. Blueberries

HAFSAH. Peanut butter and blueberries?

BILAL. Not had it before?

HAFSAH. Where'd you get it from?

---

8. He holds himself back from saying 'phenchod'.

BILAL. What d'ya mean 'get it from'?
    That's a Bilal classic – a Bilassic
    mix something soft and sweet with something crunchy –
    makes it easier to swallow
    something mitha[9] and something... bi-ttar?

They burst out laughing.

HAFSAH. Wow... bet the Pahar are really proud of the peanut-
    butter-blueberry-sandwich
    bastion of the Kashmiri palate!

BILAL. I just gave ya half my sandwich!
    Tell ya what *you* remind me of – learnt this last week:
    'bandar kyaa jane adrak ka sawaad?'

HAFSAH. What does... the monkey know about... er I dunno,
    something?
    – I better not be the monkey

BILAL. 'What does a monkey know about the taste of ginger?'

HAFSAH. You're calling *me* uncultured?

BILAL. Listen, if the joota fits yeah...

HAFSAH. The joota's gonna fit your face in a second!

Three Months (February)

In the university library.

BILAL. **This sitting together in the library thing started by
    accident
    saw her working one day and gave salaams
    there was a free desk, so I sat down**

**Next time she was at the same spot, moved over like she
    expected me,
    and after a few times it just becomes a thing don't it?**

9. 'Sweet.'

**No need to label it, but if you sit next to the same person
in the library every day
you probably spend more time with them than anyone
else**

HAFSAH *whispers.*

HAFSAH. Did I show you this?

BILAL. Please Hafs, Allah ne vaste,[10] I haven't finished your
last homework yet!

HAFSAH. Shh!
It's the government's list of 'Signs of Radicalisation' for
Prevent
– you know, the stuff they report you to police for
if your teacher, or your nurse, or basically anyone feels that
you're doing any of it

BILAL. Yeah the thing you're always going on about

(*Reading.*) 'Change in appearance, for example growing
a beard' – flipping heck
'Wearing more cultural clothes' – cultural clothes? What's
that meant to mean?
'Isolating oneself from others' – jeez

HAFSAH. You realise you do all of these?
Is it since you started hanging out with me?
Am I radicalising you?

They giggle in hushed library tones.

**The guy sitting opposite takes his headphones out – white
guy
'Some of us are trying to work?'**

**I give Bilal an eye-roll and turn back to my book, but he's
not having it**

BILAL. If you put your headphones back in you won't hear us
mate, simples

Be annoyed at me, fair play, but Hafs?

---

10. For the sake of God.

**She's the typa girl libraries are made for always working
on something – Islamophobia this, gender that, and her
novel – novella thing – submitting it to some competition**

**Point is, if you're gonna disrespect anyone in here, it
better not be Hafs**

HAFSAH. **The guy says
'doesn't seem like you want to be in the library, so maybe
you could leave?'**

BILAL. *We* could leave?

HAFSAH. Leave it Bilal

BILAL. Naaah, if anyone's leaving now it's you bro

HAFSAH. What are you doing?
What's he doing?

BILAL. Don't get shy now

HAFSAH. Bilal, stop
Bilal stands up

BILAL. Let's have it big man, what's the problem?

HAFSAH. **The guy shakes his head and starts packing up his
books**

BILAL. Here let me give you a hand

HAFSAH. **He knocks the guy's bag of books onto the floor
everything spills out and people start turning to look**

What are you doing, Bilal?
My gosh I'm so sorry – let me help you – I don't know why
he's / being so

BILAL. / 'Doesn't seem like you want to be in the library
anyway, time to move along yeah?'

HAFSAH. **I'm fuming**
Sit down Bilal, what is wrong with you?

BILAL. Phenchod

HAFSAH. **The guy leaves, me and Bilal stay standing**

What was that?

BILAL. Some people need a *smack* sometimes Hafs

HAFSAH. What are you on about?

BILAL. Guys like that need humbling

HAFSAH. What about guys like *you*?

The security guard comes over and asks if everything's okay
I tell him it's fine we're leaving and he walks away

BILAL. I'm not flipping leaving /

HAFSAH. / Well I am

She packs up and leaves. BILAL *lets out a sigh.*

BILAL. **What? We didn't do the work to be here, too? ha**
Guys like that'll see me outside this same building and ask if I'm selling
but they don't want me inside

I know what they see:
BRUM – taxi – shisha – 'gangs'
What? I can't read a book?

Nah
I ain't letting someone speak like that
especially not to her

Not to Hafs

Four Months (March)

HAFSAH *is walking to a photography exhibition in East London.* BILAL *is already there.*

HAFSAH. **Haven't spoken to him since the outburst**
   been avoiding the library
   and I was hoping he wouldn't come today
   bought the tickets weeks ago so I thought he might even
   have forgotten
   but he's standing outside as I approach the gallery

   And he's – what – he's smoking?

   Since when do you smoke?

BILAL. **Tsk**
   Asalaamualaykum wa rahmatullahi wa barakatuhu[11]

HAFSAH. **Tsk**
   Walaykum asalaam wa rahmatullahi wa barakatuhu[12]

BILAL. Didn't know you were here yet

HAFSAH. Didn't know you smoked

   BILAL *continues to smoke, slowly, carefully.*

BILAL. I do and I don't

HAFSAH. **Ugh**

BILAL. I know, it's disgusting, expensive, and it'll kill ya!

HAFSAH. I don't really want the story Bilal
   can you just not do it around me yeah?

   BILAL *takes a few more puffs then stubs the cigarette out slowly before joining her in the queue.*

BILAL. **Don't know why I've come to be honest**

---

11. This is the full version of the Islamic greeting: 'May the peace, mercy and blessings of God be upon you.'
12. It is out of Islamic etiquette that one must answer a greeting with the same or better, despite any ill feeling.

She's obviously still annoyed
and I don't have anything to say that she'll flipping like
I just can't be at mine right now, Abdulla's moved in and
it's too, it's just a lot

I love Abdulla, don't get me wrong, he's my boy
But when I'm with him I'm – I'm not the Bilal Hafsah
knows
and flipping heck, if I tried to get into WHY he's had to
move in with me
nah – she'd never get it

HAFSAH. Hani was adamant this was an Official Meet
originally
'First thing you're doing off campus? That's serious
Hafs!'
ha – if only she could see us now

Mythri on the other hand
she's completely against him now, said he's shown erratic
character,
'You need a soft boy instead,
a pious boy who writes diaspora poetry!'
I don't need a boy at all...

BILAL. Some hipster guy comes to check our tickets
I don't go to stuff like this but she invited me so

The photos remind me of my brother and my cousins
I wonder if the boys in the pictures are here
but I don't see anyone who looks as out of place as they
would

Check this one Hafs
reminds me of eating chicken and chips on the way home
from school
I used to have a scooter exactly like that no lie – loved that
thing

HAFSAH. He finds it more nostalgic than I expected
but the secular romanticising of these men just irks me
paedophiles and terrorists when it suits them, handsome
victims now

Before I can say anything
some white woman with a bob overhears us and asks
'is Bilal from Birmingham?' They start talking

I shrink, all I see is her wine glass and green earrings
bobbing up and down as she laughs at whatever he's
saying

He's not even that funny

I find myself in front of a photo of a boy who looks deep
into my eyes
He's sitting on a swing, poised, beautifully
smoke billowing out of his mouth in front of a council
estate

Caption just says *'Mohammed, sixteen'*

I wonder about Mohammed's sisters, his mum, where are
they?
Do they know he smokes?
What are they dealing with?
Where's Mohammed's dad?

BILAL. You wandered off

HAFSAH. Just looking around

BILAL. Achhaaa
    Who d'ya reckon this geezer is?
    Handsome boy ain't he?
    khush shakil-wala[13]

    Pause.

She's quiet
doesn't even ask what that means

HAFSAH. I'm wondering who his mum is actually
    where *she* is, what *she* does /

BILAL. / Probably working some eighteen-hour shift to pay off
    the mortgage his dad left behind

———————————
13. 'Good-looking' in Urdu.

and look what he's doing
how he's helping

Pause.

HAFSAH. Ironic

BILAL. **Flipping hell**
Just lay it on me Hafs

HAFSAH. What?

BILAL. You're obviously pissed off

HAFSAH. No, I'm just wondering if I really know you at all to
be honest

BILAL. Cos of a cig?
Frick's sake

> BILAL *heaves a sigh. They stay in silence looking at the
> photo for a long tense moment.*

> Know how ya said about your old man?
> How you don't chill with him and that?

HAFSAH. What's he got to do with anything?

BILAL. Is it cos, did he ever –
you know – with you, or your mum or sisters?
I'm asking cos I know how it can be

HAFSAH. What? No, never

> *Pause.* HAFSAH *is torn between engaging and refusing, she
> stays silent but we read it on her face.*

BILAL. Smoked my first cig when I was eleven
best day ever
with my brother and sister –
hadn't seen Khadj since she moved out two years before
and Danyaal, well, musta been five six years

I used to skip school and just walk for hours sometimes
one day I randomly clocked them in some park way away
from ends

both smoking
they start panicking – make me swear not to tell Dad I've
seen 'em
I say only if they let *me* have a smoke

They didn't tell me it was hash

BILAL *laughs to himself*.

Have you ever?

Nah, well they started creasing cos how bad I was coughing
Then after a while we were all creasing
Went to this cornershop and got those old-school Doritos
Danyaal nicked 'em or he made Khadj do it, can't remember

But I never wanted that day to end
to go back to that flipping
but I couldn't leave Mum alone with him

Pause.

Point is
I didn't really *stop* smoking till three years ago – in Kashmir
quit hash, ciggies, everything – even though everyone
flipping chain smokes there
I drew a clean line under my jahilliya years – started praying,
fasting, everything

Not put anything between my lips in those three years

Pause.

HAFSAH. What would you have said if you saw *me* smoking
outside when you arrived?

BILAL. Wouldn't judge ya

HAFSAH. You'd be surprised though

BILAL. Maybe a little bit

HAFSAH. *See.* Girls don't get to flaunt 'jahillya years' – 'years
of ignorance'
You say you did this and that but now it's the past and you
pray so it doesn't matter
– when do *we* get to say that? Women?

Can you imagine these photos but with girls?
Journalists wouldn't be calling that 'stunning and sombre',
it'd be an exposé
'Muslim girls gone wild'

You think you're the only one who has stuff Bilal
and that makes it okay for you to lash out at people
embarrass me in public
make your smoking into some sad story rather than just plain
offensive, which it *is*

BILAL. Oh believe me love *that's* not the sad story

HAFSAH. Go on then
Amaze me
What is it you think is so mysterious and profound that I
can't understand about your life?

BILAL. My life ain't like your Hafs

HAFSAH. No, it's not!
Cos *your* tragedy gets put up in galleries
Where's our exhibitions?

BILAL. You're crying about not being in exhibitions yeah
just be grateful you're not in the ground yet love
that's what we're crying about

HAFSAH. Oh great, a trauma contest, of course!
My dad does this too
can't see anything else for your own sob stories
he calls me an 'Islamist' cos I talk about Islamophobia

The man was in Afghanistan in the eighties, fighting in
Bosnia in the nineties
he knows what I'm talking about when I talk about injustice
but he's decided cos *he's* home now, the fight's over –
gets to say he was a mujahid, did *his* bit to protect the
Muslims
now he can sit in his room, ignore the kids,
and only come out once a day to eat the dinner that's
magically on the table for him

He doesn't care that it's not over for the rest of us
when me and my mum and sisters walk down the street we're
targets *today*
but in his eyes that's just some 'extremist' 'chip on my
shoulder'
he was the world's only real victim

HAFSAH *scoffs*.

– like you

HAFSAH *sighs*.

I only wanted you to apologise, Bilal

Girl with the bob has to cut in now of course
Civilise the barbarians
'Is everything okay over here?'

BIALAL. **Hafs says it's fine, we're just leaving**
Blondie goes to me
'aw that's a shame'
flipping hell, tryna get me killed?

HAFSAH. **I leave them to it**

BILAL. **Have to chase her out the building the speed she's**
going

HAFSAH. No please don't let *me* interrupt
go for it – she'll lap up your story mate, probably get a two-
page / spread

BILAL. / This is my *LIFE*
my brother's a flipping-
you don't even wanna know what he is /

HAFSAH. / I know what he is Bilal
I'm not stupid

BILAL*'s turn to scoff*.

BILAL. That right? You know do you?

You know what it's like to hold 10k in your hands? Cash?
Things I could do with money like that, Hafs

he tried giving it me just before I moved here
but I told him I'm not taking it, fully haram

There in his flipping blacked-out A3, cruising round like he's
saved the day
where was this generosity when Dad left Mum?
where was this cash when the next guy left?

Know what he said?
I ever question him like that again I'll end up in hospital or in
the ground
and he's not joking Hafs, he's capable of that

You *don't* know what he is.

Pause.

HAFSAH. Fine.
You win.
I *don't* understand your life
I don't understand *you*
You have it worst of everyone
there's your get-out clause
Happy?

Is that what you want me to say?

Four Months and a Quarter (April)

SOAS Library.

BILAL. **Can't sleep properly this week**
partly Abdulla taking up half the bed – though he gets me
up for fajr to be fair
but it's mainly, keep thinking about what she said

She's avoiding my calls so I've come to the library
knew she'd be here
but she's with flipping Mythri who gives me absolute

lethal looks whenever she sees me
just my luck

HAFSAH. **Mythri says 'Don't look but he's over there'**
I look
he gives me a timid smile
Mythri says 'Don't you dare smile back, remember what
Hani said?'

I don't smile, but not cos of Hani
all she said was, 'He needs to sort himself out'
and she's right
I've said my bit, I don't get the guy, don't get what he
wants

BILAL. **Abdulla told me I'd have to embarrass myself to get**
her to talk to me
but I wasn't prepared for The Mighty Flipping Mythri

(*Quietly, to himself.*) Bismillah

I walk up slow
feel like the whole library's watching
and Mythri's not going anywhere
flip's sake

Hey, ah, salaams Hafs, can I talk to you for a second, alone,
please?

She doesn't even let Hafs reply
'Whatever you want to say you can say in front of me'

HAFSAH. **I don't contradict Mythri**
just say, Walaykum asalaam

BILAL. **Flipping hell we're doing this yeah?**

Hafs – I just wanted to er check we're good yeah?

Mythri goes 'Good? Wow!'

I'm sorry okay!
– for what happened at the exhibition
I know I was... being obnoxious, you were right

HAFSAH. Mythri 'pftttss' at that
I want to too
but – I could never tell *her* this –
I feel a bit sorry for him
I *did* dismiss a lot of what he said, and some of that stuff
was heavy

I ask Mythri to give us a minute

She gives me a look and walks about five steps away

BILAL. **Thinks she's paid security this girl**

Look, Hafs, I've had time to think about everything and
you're right
I'm not – sometimes I just get so inside my own head it's
like –
it's what you said
I don't flipping think about other people

HAFSAH. I nod slowly to make him wait
I'm not gonna say it's not true
been a long time coming

but then I make sure to lower my voice so Mythri can't
hear
I'm sorry as well

BILAL. What you sorry for?

HAFSAH. I was harsher than I meant to be
and I didn't know the full extent to be honest
about your brother and/

BILAL. / Nah, sometimes the truth is harsh innit?

Beat.

I er didn't know about your dad
was he really in Afghanistan? Bosnia?

HAFSAH. Before he married my mum

BILAL. Must be an interesting guy

HAFSAH. I guess he is a *bit* – he's why I love to read
used to leave books on my bed every week
our only interaction

BILAL. What kind of books?

HAFSAH. Everything, Che Guevara's *Motorcycle Diaries* – that
was the first one
Ali Shariati, Sayid Qutb, Mawdudi, Fanon, Cesaire, Iqbal

BILAL. Properrrr anti-imperialist yeah?

Mythri coughs loudly
But Hafs gives her a look to say it's okay
Have that on your chips Mythri!

HAFSAH. That's why I don't get this 'put up and shut up'
attitude

He's renounced everything nowadays
no God, no purpose, nothing

BILAL. No God?

HAFSAH. I know.
Allah guide him
– and all of us to be honest

BILAL. **I can feel Mythri literally burning holes in the side**
of my head

HAFSAH. What are you doing tonight?

BILAL. **Got a term's worth of Urdu vocab to memorise for**
my exam tomorrow
Nothing

HAFSAH. I've got the er – residency announcement

BILAL. For the New York thing?

HAFSAH. Yeah
I won't get it but – I have to go
Do you wanna meet me after?

***

BILAL. **I wait for her in a cafe near Old Street**
told Abdulla she's talking to me again
musta sounded too gassed cos he said, 'Don't be catching
feelings bro
you've got your mum to think about'

It's not as if I've called Mum in weeks, but I know why he
said it
last time I was home she told me she wants to get married
again
have someone to help her out
I thought, flipping hell am I that useless?

HAFSAH. **It's raining hard**
the type where I wish my glasses had windscreen wipers
my coat is meant to be waterproof but I feel rain seeping
into my sleeves

I throw myself into the café doorway and catch my breath
It's warm and dry and smells of hot chocolate and
goodness
And then he's there, in front of me

BILAL. Salaam alaykum
What you saying?
You're soaking!

HAFSAH. Bilal, guess what?

BILAL. **She looks at me with such openness**
soaked through and glistening with rain
got this expression that makes me feel /

HAFSAH. / I got it! The New York residency!

BILAL. Oh shit serious?

HAFSAH. Yeah! I applied so long ago now I just assumed it'd
never happen
– I can finally finish my novella

BILAL. Shabaash! Kya baath hai![14]
MashaAllah man – we gotta celebrate – what do you want? –
It's on me

---

14. 'Well done! Bravo!' In Urdu.

HAFSAH. You sure?

BILAL. Course I am! New York baby!

HAFSAH. **As I read the board he reaches towards my face
with both hands
before I can register what's happening he's taking my
glasses off**

**Doesn't look at me
just wipes the water away with this tenderness
like it's just instinct
like that's just what we do**

**I try to focus on my order
he glances at me with a smile**

Er – hot chocolate and a flapjack please

**When I turn back he's holding the glasses out for me to
lean into
his hands are the closest to my face they've ever been
I'm holding my breath
can't move my arms**

BILAL. New flipping York yeah?
That's another level
Can't believe I'm about to say this Hafs but you're no longer
dunya-ke-becharay

HAFSAH. God knows what I am now

Makes me wonder, did my grandparents go through all that
for me to write sci-fi
in some all-expenses-paid-for New York trip?

BILAL. Arguably, yeah?
They were surviving – that's not a dream Hafs

You writing in New York though, that's proper *living*

HAFSAH. I am excited, I am but
when I looked around the room at all these artsy people I just
thought, god,
who does this help? Isn't it all a bit dunya-oriented?
How's it bringing me closer to God?

And what if they gave me it because they want me to write
some story about being saved from an honour-killer dad
or falling in love with a white boy?
taking my hijab off, losing my religion, same old same old

BILAL. You'd never write that

Pause.

(*Tenderly.*) You ever think about the future Hafs?

HAFSAH. Doesn't everyone?

BILAL. Yeah but like, you ever think about who'd be there?

HAFSAH. Aliens and stuff? AI? Imam Mahdi?
All the time! You know I do, that's what this whole novella's
about

BILAL. **Flipping hell**

No, not – never mind

Beat.

Don't know anyone who's ever been to New York you know
Will you send me a postcard?

HAFSAH. With Homeland Security reading it?

BILAL. Oi you're not that big of a deal

HAFSAH. My dad's a mujahid you know!

They laugh.

BILAL. You're going *after* Ramadan yeah?

HAFSAH. Yeah, not till July

BILAL. They do big iftaris anywhere in London?

Even better – why don't you come round for iftari at mine
one day?
not just me – Abdulla would be there too – my er flatmate

HAFSAH. That sounds doable
Doable?

How about some time end of next week?
I know
I know
but Mythri's not here right now, okay

Four Months and Three Quarters (April)

Bilal's house.

HAFSAH. **Look, it's just a –**
There's a third person there, it's totally –
and it's Ramadan
it's not like that anyway
I even told my sisters about it – kind of

Mythri said I'm a lost cause
Hani says she can't advise me any more cos everyone
deletes Muzmatch in Ramadan, this is out of the realm of
her expertise

I knock
An extremely tall man answers the door

Hi – erm is this – I'm looking for Bilal?

He says 'Asalaamualykum', his name is Abdulla, and
come in – Bilal's just cooking
doesn't make eye contact
I thank him and shuffle in

Asalaamualaykum – I brought these
I pass a box of dates to Bilal

BILAL. Walaykum asalaam, amazing
I'm making daal, hope that's okay?
Mum says you're not meant to feed guests daal but it's my
best recipe

HAFSAH. Nah, I'm down with that, healthy

BILAL. **Didn't wanna go overboard**
can't have Abdulla thinking I'm making special effort
daal's just daal right?
Though Abdulla's made it clear he thinks this entire thing
is special effort
said he's not leaving the room at *any* point, and I said,
good, that's the whole idea

This is Abdulla – Abdulla, Hafs
Sorry he's a bit of a weirdo, doesn't get out much

HAFSAH. **Abdulla asks what country the dates are from**
which throws me
I double check – Egypt
Turns out Abdulla is also Egyptian which unexpectedly
warms him to me

BILAL. **They're getting on really well**
better than anticipated

flipping funny to me cos they couldn't be more different
but they don't know that yet, so I don't let on

But then Abdulla puts his foot right in it
Hafs asks what sort of housemate I am and he says – his
words – I'm 'a woman'

I see MA-Gender-Studies-Hafsah clock it
but she doesn't go interrogation-mode like she goes on me
Instead, she makes him do it himself, it's genius

Plays dumb, goes,

HAFSAH. What does that mean?

BILAL. **Abdulla says I'm a woman cos I cook and wash the**
dishes
Hafs asks

HAFSAH. Do you think those are defining parts of
womanhood?

BILAL. **I can tell he barely understands the question but he**
says 'yeah'

HAFSAH. Can a man not wash up and cook?

BILAL. **He says men should be working**

HAFSAH. Is that not work?

BILAL. **He starts to fumble**

HAFSAH. You know, the Prophet sallalahu-alayhi-wassalam
used to do housework

  – it's funny how people these days expect women to do all
the housework and work outside the home, but then say its
men whose defining characteristic is work

BILAL. **She says it like she's just noticed how strange a
contradiction it is**

  I have to avoid eye contact

  **Abdulla opens a window then turns back round with this
look**
**he thinks whatever he's about to say next is a trump card
goes, 'are you a feminist then?'**

HAFSAH. **Abdulla is low-hanging fruit for me**

  **I reserve my energy for higher-stakes discussions these
days**
But, can't lie, I've missed this
I'd go harder on an out-and-out akhi
but this guy seems sweet, and it's Ramadan
so I let him tangle himself in his own logic

  **When he throws down his trump card, asks 'am I
a feminist',**
I ask, do you think I am?

  He takes a long time to consider
pours water into three glasses
then says, 'you seem very independent'

  I ask what he makes of that
**he decides 'it's a good thing actually cos these days
men don't want to marry women who rely on them for
everything'**

I try hard not to roll my eyes,
'Okay, don't you think that makes me a man though?'

He goes very still, then makes eye contact for the first time and cracks into a smile
he knows what's happened here and I grin back

But then he comes to his own defence by moving the bar completely
Says 'okay fine, but did you know Bilal thinks mosques shouldn't be segregated?'

BILAL. I said I don't think they *have* to be in the way they are sometimes!

HAFSAH. **Abdulla says 'That's crazy'**
I say, 'You do know that in the Prophet sallalhu alayhi wasallam's mosque there was just one big area with a front and back, not separate spaces altogether?'

He says, 'Fine, but they were the best of people, they could manage that!'
Why couldn't *we* 'manage' that?
He says, 'men have filthy minds, they can't be trusted'

Abdulla, I hate to tell you this but *you're* starting to sound like a feminist

BILAL. **Hafs is having a ball**

Gets Abdulla into a corner where he basically admits that if women pray behind him, he'll end up trying to look at them through his legs

I'm creasing and Hafs says, 'that sounds like something you need to work out with Allah rather than build an outhouse for women'

Abdulla goes red but I can see he rates her

HAFSAH. **Magrib comes in and we open our fasts**
I ask to pray in my own room somewhere please
don't want Abdulla doing gymnastics

BILAL. **When we come down to eat, I feel a weird sense of cosiness**

The three of us just vibing
like a little family
I know that sounds weird but –
I've always felt that with Abdulla, and with Hafs there,
dunno, just feels right

HAFSAH. **Abdulla tells Bilal he's put too much salt in the**
daal again

BILAL. It's proportionate!

HAFSAH. **Abdulla says:**

BILAL. **'Proportions like this is why you failed accountancy**
bro'

HAFSAH. Hang on, failed? That's a different story from what
I've heard!

BILAL. It was a joint decision to leave!

HAFSAH. Hmm, sounds 'joint' like the 'joint' decision to
partition India

BILAL. **I remind Abdulla he's a *guest* in my house**
tell Hafs he's not actually my flatmate,
just been staying with me a few weeks to get his head
sorted
– we've known each other forever, grew up in Brum
together, basically brothers

hope she'll understand that's why I put up with his BS

HAFSAH. **Turns out Abdulla's more like a brother to Bilal**
he's come to stay in London for a breather
though then I realise 'a breather' actually means
something else

Both Abdulla's parents died in the Egyptian revolution –
he says it quickly
shot by police in the 2011 protests when they were visiting
back home

The reason he's staying in London with Bilal now
is that Abdulla's brother
– the one he lived with in Birmingham since the parents died –
his only brother – only family
was stabbed

'So I'm staying here, working for Just Eat for now' he says
moving swiftly on

BILAL. Hafs's face is heavy
I can't do anything cos I didn't expect Abdulla to talk about it
he never talks about this stuff even with me

But he's going and going
not deep but not stopping either

Then he brings up my brother, Danyaal
just in passing, just part of the story
obviously thinks she knows, and I can't stop him cos it's already happening

He goes, 'the funny thing is,
before I came to London, Danyaal actually offered me a job'

'Doing what he does!?' – Abdulla's getting mad now
'Don't get it twisted, I didn't say no cos of some ethical shit,
but I wasn't about to work for the guy who put my brother in the ground'

There is silence. They freeze.

HAFSAH. I look at Bilal, he looks away
my brain's rushing to catch up
his Danyaal, *his* brother?

Abdulla senses the change
looks from me to Bilal
puts his head in his hands, 'bro, you coulda told me she didn't know'

I feel like I'm supposed to say something
my chest is tightening

(*Slowly.*) **Bilal's Danyaal stabbed Abdulla's brother, and
they both know
and they're both here
and I'm here
I'm supposed to react**

BILAL. **She doesn't say anything**

HAFSAH. **I have to say something**

BILAL. **She's just looking at us**

HAFSAH. **I'm supposed to say something**

I er, didn't

She coughs.

That's so

BILAL. **Me and Abdulla start speaking at the same time
just want her to stop speaking
not say sorry**

**She gives me this look that makes the back of my throat
burn
I get up and start washing the dishes**

HAFSAH. **Abdulla starts speaking about something else
somehow
but I'm barely listening, just watching Bilal, useless**

**He lights a cigarette
Abdulla says, 'I thought you were gonna quit that shit for
Ramadan'**

BILAL. I was

HAFSAH. **The conversation doesn't revive itself after that
Abdulla wants to go to mosque for taraavi
Bilal walks me to the station**

Beat.

BILAL. Thanks for coming, Hafs
   Sorry Abdulla's so /

HAFSAH. / No, I really like him – surprisingly

BILAL. Yeah, he's an idiot but, I knew you'd see the best in him
   Pause.

HAFSAH. I'm sorry if you didn't want me to / know

BILAL. / No it's not like that
   I just never
   I have no idea where to start sometimes Hafs

HAFSAH. I get it now,
   why you've been/

BILAL. / I shoulda told you, you of all people

HAFSAH. You don't have to explain

BILAL. I didn't really know my dad
   just a few prison visits on Eid and stuff
   only Danyaal remembered what things had been like before
   Dad went pen
   he told Mum to leave Dad when he got out
   told Dad our uncle was more of a father to us

   But Dad went ballistic
   I'd never seen that kind of anger before
   physically lifted and threw Danyaal out the house
   dashed his stuff out our bedroom window – glass all over my
   bed
   Mum couldn't do nothing – couldn't call the police
   I was only six but even *I* knew the house was full of uncle's
   stuff –
   Dad was only ever a pusher, uncle was the real one behind it
   all
   used our house sometimes – Danyaal looked after gear for
   him
   so police were out the question

   He gave me a little fist bump when he left, told me to be
   good to Mum

I remember thinking it weren't fair, he'd got it better than me
getting to stay with uncle and leaving me with this guy I
didn't hardly know

But now I'm here and he is what he is, isn't he?
Not really his fault, but what does that matter to Abdulla's
brother?

Pause.

I'm scared to look her in the eye
don't wanna see pity for being such a bleeding –
but instead, she's looking at me in this way I've never
seen anyone look at me

I wish I wasn't such a flipping coward
cos I know how rare this is, but I'm not what she/

HAFSAH. / Thank you for trusting me, it means a lot

I don't know what Abdulla's going through but er

Pause, we feel that she wants to say something more.

we all know what it's like to lose someone don't we?

Tender pause.

I'm glad he's got you, and you have each other

Are you gonna be okay?

BILAL. Course, are you?

She nods a yes.

HAFSAH. Insha'Allah

I'm going home till after Eid but, you can call me anytime

BILAL. Thanks Hafs

Six Months (June)

Sunny. Central London.

BILAL. **I've never celebrated birthdays**
   not even from a religious perspective
   just no one made a big deal of 'em growing up

   She invited me to hers – some sort of picnic with her
   mates
   but I knew The Mighty Mythri would be there so had to
   make my excuses
   told her we'd do something the next day, before she goes
   to New York

   Her sisters gave her a Polaroid and she's excited to use
   for the first time
   we get the bus to Piccadilly Circus like proper tourists
   she tells me to take a selfie of us – my arms are longer

HAFSAH. **I always remember that photo**
   waiting for it to develop stood under the stoop of a shop
   front we could never afford to go in

   We watched the colour seep into our smiles
   and he said it made him feel like he was finally living his
   adult life
   the sort of photo people in films have of themselves
   to show they exist outside the film plot

   I knew what he meant, didn't say that though
   instead – stupidly – I said

   You can have it if you want?

BILAL. Your first ever Polaroid?

HAFSAH. A gift

BILAL. Aren't you supposed to be getting gifts not giving 'em?

HAFSAH. Well you know how I feel about social norms

BILAL. **I hold it in my hand and look between it and her**

HAFSAH. You can't lose it!
   I might want to see it in the future, might change my mind!

BILAL. Alright alright

HAFSAH. **He pulls out his wallet and puts it in that bit, you know the see-through part?**

BILAL. A whole month yeah?

HAFSAH. Why, you gonna miss me?

BILAL. Don't get gassed
   you better bring me a worthy souvenir though

HAFSAH. I'll get you some proper Amreekan peanut butter for your Kashmiri classic

BILAL. Now we're talking!

   They laugh.

HAFSAH. Bilal, can I say something?

BILAL. We're already saying things aren't we? What?
   Don't make me nervous

HAFSAH. No it's just, I'm going away so I thought I should just –

   You know how me and you are and everything?
   Obviously you know that I like you
   but erm, full cards on the table, just in case it's not obvious
   I just wanted to let you know that I really like you

   Pause.

BILAL. How d'ya mean?

HAFSAH. No… you can't do that
   You *know* what I mean

BILAL. 'Really like me'?
   I *really like* peanut butter and blueberry sarnies

HAFSAH. **What I say next isn't even for him, this is for me**

   Have you ever watched *Dirty Dancing*?

BILAL. No?

HAFSAH. Good, you shouldn't, it's totally inappropriate

> But there's a scene in it where she says to him
> 'I'm scared of walking out of this room and never feeling the
> rest of my whole life the way I feel when I'm with you'
>
> And *that* is basically what I mean when I say 'really like you'
>
> **Oh my god did I just say that?**
> Sorry – I don't know why I –
> that was so extra
> you don't have to say anything I just thought since I'm
> leaving I should say it
> but I don't want it to / seem as if

BILAL. / Are you gonna let me speak?

HAFSAH. Oh, right, sorry

BILAL. Flipping heck Hafs,
obviously I've been thinking the same thing
– not the dodgy dancing bit but

HAFSAH. Dirty

BILAL. Right – sorry can we sit down?

HAFSAH. **We sit down on a bench and he shuffles away
from me**

BILAL. **Butterflies, gotta keep my distance**

HAFSAH. Are you saying you feel the same?

BILAL. **My heart's beating fast real fast**

HAFSAH. **I can hear the blood whooshing through my body
everything is too loud
I'm so aware of my limbs, my skin, my face**

BILAL. Yeah, I guess I do
I do feel the same

*They look at each other for a long moment, the air is thick
and completely transparent at the same time.*

But, Hafs, what would you want to happen now?

HAFSAH. Well it's not complicated – I already spoke to my
    sisters about it and
    I guess we just, tell our mums
    keep getting to know each other
    and
    get married at some point I guess

    Pause.

BILAL. I thought you said marriage is all rowing and fights

HAFSAH. Well I'd do it different, more like the sunnah

BILAL. Hafs, I was gonna say something to you before
    back when you got the residency
    But I didn't cos I –

    You gotta understand
    what I feel for you is what everyone says you're meant to

    But I don't think it's responsible
    for me to bring – not just you but anyone – into my…
    situation

HAFSAH. *Situation*?
    Come on, don't be cliché, this isn't *Romeo and Juliet*

BILAL. It's not straightforward

HAFSAH. What do you mean specifically?
    This doesn't come every day you know

BILAL. I know, I've got butterflies right now Hafs
    you're amazing, you're a special woman
    but I've gotta have priorities
    All the men in my family have just pissed off and done what
    they want
    my dad, Danyaal
    there's only me left

    When I was home at Eid Mum couldn't even get the day off
    work
    the mortgage is killing her Hafs – no wonder interest is
    flipping haram

I *shoulda* stuck to accountancy
I gotta step up

HAFSAH. You don't put off being with the right person cos of
a *mortgage*
you're supposed to just *do* it,
I don't even understand how / that's

BILAL. / I'm meant to be financially –
like, what flipping job can I even get with an area-studies
degree?

HAFSAH. It feels like you're trying to find obstacles

BILAL. My whole life is a flipping obstacle Hafs

   BILAL *puts his head in his hands and slumps.*

   I failed the Urdu exam

HAFSAH. What? How??

BILAL. And I still need to learn flipping Pahari

HAFSAH. Okay one thing at a / time

BILAL. / I met a guy in Kashmir, have I told you this?

HAFSAH. What?

BILAL. Grew up here like us but he spoke Pahari perfectly
Guess why?

HAFSAH. No idea

BILAL. Married a woman from back home

   Beat.

HAFSAH. Riiight
So what are you –
are you saying –
you think wanting to learn a *language* should inform who
you marry?

BILAL. It's important Hafs /

HAFSAH. / You think it would be better to *ruin* some Kashmiri
girl's life by making her marry *you* – an English guy who

makes a dilemma out of what degree he's doing in *London*
and make her be your *teacher* cos of your red passport
privilege?

You're saying *that* is preferable to *this*?

HAFSAH *scoffs*.

Anyone can learn a language Bilal!
I can learn Pahari!
People have been learning languages through human history!
It's a language!

BILAL. It's a dying dialect

HAFSAH. You're always gonna be from Birmingham, Bilal
not the Pahar, not the Pothwari plateau
THIS is your life
it's not out there waiting for you
It's right here
I'm right here
give me a straight answer

BILAL *stays silent*.

you shouldn't have kept spending time with me
you shouldn't have got to know me

BILAL. Hafs –

HAFSAH. No if you knew you felt this way, that you couldn't
be with me then /

BILAL. / I didn't know!
I didn't expect this Hafs

HAFSAH *scoffs*.

HAFSAH. You spend every day with me, work with me
invite me to your house to meet your childhood best friend
tell me things you say you've never told anyone, put my
picture in your wallet

You started this Bilal, you came into *my* life
I never texted you back for a *reason*
I don't *let* people in

HAFSAH *is choked up*.

BILAL. I don't know what to say

Long pause.

HAFSAH. When I prayed istakhara[15] last night about telling you
I really thought to myself, there's only two ways this can go
either you say you don't feel the same and I suck it up
or you say you do and we get married

Not this
not *this*

Pause.

**I actually considered what I'd do if he asked me to stay
today
If he asked me not to go on the residency, not go to New
York**

(*Choked up*.) **I would have stayed**
I* would have stayed for a *man

pathetic

BILAL. **I can't look her in the eye
I can see it so close in front of me but /**

HAFSAH. / Great well I guess I'll just get my bus home, thanks
for the birthday surprise

BILAL. Hafs – Hafs man don't

---

15. Prayer for making a decision and putting the affair into God's hands
to make it easy if it's good for you, and avert it from you if it is not
good for you.

Seven Months (July)

A phone rings. HAFSAH *is in New York,* BILAL *is on a train.*

HAFSAH. **New York isn't London**
Don't get me wrong, it's big and anonymising, a place to
get lost in
but a bit too lost
in London I still know the street corners
but here it's hard to hold onto anything

And he's not here
I know that's tragic
I've tried not to think about him
Hani and Mythri said it's better this way cos I can be
fully present here now
and I guess they're right, there's a lot to distract myself
with

The institute is beautiful, and I write overlooking this
amazing park every day
write six hours and walk everywhere I can in between
spend my expenses on bagels and cheesecakes and
anything New York-y
watch shows and poetry and stand-up in the evenings
find a new mosque as often as I can

But he hasn't even *tried* to call me, not once
And every day it's harder to distract myself

So when his name lights up my screen I can't help but
think *finally*

Phone rings.

Bilal?

BILAL. Hafs I'm sorry to call I just
I didn't know who else to /

HAFSAH. / Is everything okay?

BILAL. I'm on the train Hafs
left my bag for just a few minutes

Told the woman next to me, 'can you watch this'
while I went to the toilet
but I took a bit of time cos I was tryna make wudhu[16] in that
tiny fricking space

Anyway, as I'm finishing I start hearing a commotion
go back in and the woman with my bag points at me
other people standing up
she goes 'that's him'

I swear to God, Hafs, *kasm*
people start *physically* moving away from me – backing
away

She goes 'that's his bag!'
someone's like, 'I'm gonna ring the British Transport Police!'

I get my bag
get right up in the woman's face
say, 'What are you doing? I just asked if you could watch my
bag!'

She says, flipping hell, she goes,
'I won't be threatened by you!' and starts *crying*

Well, you know how that goes
so I back out of there quick
but this one guy goes, 'show us what's in the bag,
Mohammed' /

HAFSAH. / Wow /

BILAL. / I give him the finger
say, 'you wanna see what's inside yeah? Wait and see'
cos I'm pissed off
I know it was stupid but that flipping woman –

I've walked down to the other end of the train but I don't
know what to do now Hafs
that's why I'm –

---

16. Ablution.

I'm sorry I know I shouldn't –
you probably don't wanna hear from me /

HAFSAH. / How long till you get off?

BILAL. I'm so flipping tired Hafs

He sighs and holds back his emotions.

Erm – fifteen minutes

HAFSAH. Okay, look, when you get off – just /

BILAL. / I think they actually called the transport police
they're gonna be there when I get off aren't they?

Flipping 'see it, say it, sorted'
What do I do?

HAFSAH. It's okay!
You haven't done anything!
Not that that's – but I doubt they'll be there

BILAL. You didn't see the way they were looking at me

HAFSAH. Just be confident, walk out as normal
If they try and speak to you, you're supposed to ask –
Oh god I'm trying to remember from my – 'under what
powers am I being stopped'? Okay?

Cos I don't think the transport police can arrest – oh, wait,
they can –
but you don't have to speak to them okay?

Do not speak to them, okay? Bilal?

BILAL. Flipping hell

HAFSAH. It's okay it'll be fine insha'Allah

BILAL. Shit what time is it for you?

HAFSAH. Fiveish in the morning
But it's –
it doesn't matter /

BILAL. / Sorry Hafs, I just didn't know who else to /

HAFSAH. / let me text Younis as a precaution
he's got numbers for lawyers for this kind of thing

and get their badge numbers, okay?

I'll stay on the line don't worry

BILAL. **She stays on the line for the next fifteen minutes**
I don't even know what we talk about or if we do
all I remember is her telling me to read ayatul-kursi, I do

I don't know anything else but that I'm raging, furious
her being on the other end is the only thing keeping me
contained

Pause.

The train pulls in
my heart's so loud, I need water
get off and try and walk normal
but you know when you try and now you look more
suspect?

End of the platform I see 'em
three pigs pointing at the train
talking in their radios, shit

Hear Hafs in my ear saying just walk slow, head high
but I've been here before, it don't work
she don't know this routine like I do

I stop listening, duck round the other side as if I'm
waiting for another train
take off my hoodie
shove it in my bag
keep watching

Hafs's asking me something
don't reply
can't focus
they're waiting for me
I start walking
and then, shit

HAFSAH. Bilal?

I go to the window
voices ask him to move off the platform

I'm trying to remind him and he does
I think he says, 'under what powers?'

But the line's not clear

I press my forehead against the glass
They say – I think they say – 'we just want to chat'

He says he doesn't want to chat
voices start rising, rustling
I'm cramming my phone as far up to my ear as it can go
eyes scrunched closed in case it helps me hear better

Bilal?

The line goes dead

Long pause.

I keep calling
I know he can't, won't answer, probably
But I keep calling

my whole body's shaking
the sky begins to pale, I pray fajr
keep calling
watch the sky turn pink over Brooklyn, say my adhkaar[17]

I know he's probably fine but I check in case he ever sent
me his mum's number
he didn't
why would he?

Open my laptop, keep calling
31,124 the word count blinks
they say that's a good length for a novella

---

17. Plural of 'dhikr' – meaning 'remembrances of God.' Specifically
in this context: a morning and evening litany of glorification is
recommended with prayers and sayings from the Quran and prophetic
narrations.

'one of the most prolific writers we've ever had' they told
me yesterday
'all that in twenty days'

I keep calling
don't leave my apartment
tell the hosts I feel sick, I do

Can't write
can't think who to contact
search key words in Twitter
'Euston' 'arrest' @britishtransportpolice
Facebook search Abdulla – no account
think about messaging Mythri, or Hani, don't
keep calling

I start replaying Bilal telling me he didn't expect this – us
think of all the things we say we don't expect
even though they were always there

think about the fact he rang me out of everyone he knows
and I'm still here
I still answered

The sky turns dark again
I sit in the window
keep calling him
don't sleep, open my laptop
31,124 – a good novella

Good for what?

Nine Months (August)

Hampstead Heath.

HAFSAH. **He said to meet at the top of Hampstead Heath
cos there's no signal up there**

BILAL. **I stop a few feet away**
feel like I'm seeing her for the first time
give myself a second before I say
Asalaamu alaykum Hafsah from Bradford Sharif

HAFSAH. **He says my name like it belongs to another time**
looks thinner – can you lose weight that fast?
His eyes are darting more than even before
Walaykum asalaam Bilal

BILAL. Glad ya decided to come back yaara

HAFSAH. I was always coming back

BILAL. Early though

HAFSAH. I couldn't focus after the –
had enough anyway – homesick

BILAL. **Neither of us knows what to say**
we sit down

HAFSAH. How are you doing?
You look rough

BILAL. You can't say that Hafs, I got a fresh trim to see you!

I'm alright now though
alhamdulilah kulli haal[18]

What about you, big fish?
What's New York saying?

HAFSAH. I was so worried Bilal
rang you for two days straight
tried Twitter, Facebook, everything
I even prayed istakhara about contacting your mum!
I know you explained a bit in your email, but my mind's just /
been

BILAL. / It ain't no biggie Hafs, they said I was being
uncooperative
I said what you told me – under what powers was I being
stopped?

18. 'Praise is due to God in every state', in Arabic. An Islamic saying.

They said they had suspicion to believe I was there to
'terror-related intent', I think

HAFSAH. Serious?

BILAL. Cos of when I said to the guy, 'wait and see'
That's 'reasonable suspicion' that I was planning something
apparently
some shit like that

HAFSAH. So what? Then what did they? /

BILAL. / Said they were gonna search me
In front of the whole of Euston?
But I shoulda let them – ended up having to go to the station
instead

**I don't know how much to say
her jaw is rock solid**

They went through my phone obviously, that's why I dashed
it
laptop's probably wired now

HAFSAH. How long were you there?
I should have sent you that number – I didn't even /

BILAL. / Don't worry

HAFSAH. How am I supposed to not worry?
Look at you, you're not okay

Does your mum know?

BILAL. Well – she didn't, but some pigs have been sniffing
round ends asking about me
apparently – went to the takeaway Abdulla used to work at

HAFSAH. So she found out? Your mum?

BILAL. Well – Danyaal found out, started a whole drama
'endangering the business'
what if they'd put out a warrant to search Mum's house?
God knows what they might have found

HAFSAH. They can't do that without arresting you

BILAL. They do what they want don't they?

HAFSAH. You should have told me, Bilal!
I know people who work on this stuff from my research –
you know I do!
It sounds like they used Section 43 to search you but
what did they say when they released you?

You need legal advice
we need to talk to Younis
I texted him yesterday and –
You didn't say anything at the station did you?

Bilal?

He rolls onto his back and puts his arms behind his head

BILAL. I just wanna go man

HAFSAH. Go where?

BILAL. **I'm not looking at her but I can feel her eyes on my face
can't look at her**

Beat.

D'you –
in the future d'ya want kids?

HAFSAH. Kids?

BILAL. *I* want kids definitely insha'Allah, do you?

HAFSAH. Yeah... but /

BILAL. / That's good

Beat.

HAFSAH. Bilal did you speak to anyone?

BILAL. Know what I've been thinking?

I roll onto my side now so I face her

How d'ya feel about sending them abroad?

HAFSAH. Sending who abroad?

My kids?

He just looks at me

BILAL. Hear me out
I ain't bringing kids up here, I'm not
never wanted to, but *now*?
I'm either moving abroad or they're getting sent abroad

HAFSAH. Where is it you think there's some kind of safe haven
from this kind of thing?
And your kids' mum is just fine with you sending them
abroad?

BILAL. I'm asking her innit?

Pause, HAFSAH *shakes her head and sighs.*

HAFSAH. Bilal
the last time we spoke about this you made your position
very clear
now you're talking to me about children?

BILAL. **She lays down on** *her* **back now**
keeps her arms straight by her sides and I hear all the air
leave her

Copy her
both looking up at this grey island's clouds

Know what I kept thinking about?
When they went through all my stuff?
phone, wallet, laptop, keys, everything
That photo, Hafs, the Polaroid
how you said I had to keep it safe
how you're gonna be flipping mad at me if they take it

He sits up.

I was being a –
I was being stupid before Hafs
and maybe you've changed your mind but
I'm gonna take the risk ya haven't, cos you're here

and in all this BS Hafs, you're something
like when I rang you – I could suddenly – you make things
make sense

Hafs?

HAFSAH. **I stay quiet
stay lying down**

BILAL. Hafs?

HAFSAH. Yeah?

BILAL. Say something

HAFSAH. Okay. What's stopping you?

BILAL. Stopping me?

She sits up.

HAFSAH. Danyaal? Pahari? Your mum's mortgage?

BILAL. Those things *are* all there, they're still there I can't lie
but
I can't do it on my own

HAFSAH. So you changed your mind *now* cos you don't wanna
be alone?

BILAL. No! Hafs!
I'm fine on my own, I've *been fine* on my own
If it wasn't *you* I wouldn't be interested

I've had a *lot* of time to think
and I know that I want this now
you, us

Ten Months (September)

HAFSAH. **We found one of those unexpected mosques
he's outside waiting at the café next door, grinning**

No – not funny

BILAL. Shoe cupboard?

HAFSAH. Worse – couldn't even hear the Imam
and the two aunties with me wouldn't stand shoulder-to-
shoulder for some reason

so I'm there like some wide-winged chicken trying to close the gap

BILAL *laughs*.

Not funny!

BILAL. Can't lie Hafs that was one of the nicest mosques I've ever been in

HAFSAH. Course it was

BILAL. Are ya mad?

HAFSAH. Aren't you?

BILAL. Alright let's make dua for the masajid

HAFSAH. Great let's make dua and do nothing practical

BILAL. I'm being serious

HAFSAH. I am too!

BILAL. What do you want me to do? Start a petition?

HAFSAH. Is it so inconceivable that you, a *man* might petition a mosque for better women's space?

BILAL. Hafs –

HAFSAH. No go on – you make your dua, let's hear it

BILAL. **Flipping hell**

They both raise their hands. HAFSAH *violently,* BILAL *cautious.*

Okay um
Bismillah
allahumma salli ala sayidnaa muhamadin wa ala alihi wa sahbihi wa sallim
Allah we ask you to grant us mosques which are spacious and open to everyone
with proper space for women
and er to rid us of our arrogance

and reward those who are excluded for their sabr[19]
Ameen

Beat.

HAFSAH. Ameen
Suck-up

**The waiter brings us a pot of mint tea for two
as he leaves Bilal moves the ashtray**

BILAL. Disgusting habit

HAFSAH. Couldn't agree more

BILAL. I'm done fully, don't worry
only do it when I'm stressed

HAFSAH. So fully done, or done till you're stressed again?

BILAL. I'm not gonna be stressed again

They look at each other and burst out laughing.

BILAL prepares himself in a self-conscious way.

HAFSAH. What's happening?

BILAL. Ta'aruf rog ho jaye
to iska bhoolna behtar

Ta'aluq bojh bun jaye
to iska todna achha

Woh afsaana jisse anjaam tak laana na ho mumkin
use ek khoobsurat mod de kar chodna achha

' HAFSAH. Wow – translation please?

BILAL. It's from a poem we had to learn for this year
means, if an acquaintanceship, I guess you'd say
if it becomes difficult then 'bhoolna behtar' – better to forget

And if a friendship becomes, burdensome, let's say
then better to leave it

---

19. 'Patience, perseverance' in Arabic.

Then, that story…
er, that story which can't be brought to a natural sort of…
end

That story's better left, at a beautiful turning point

Pause.

HAFSAH. If that's your way of ending things mate, you're
literally insane

BILAL. No no no, that's me and this language pursuit – Urdu,
Pahari

Not been anything but trouble and difficulty
So maybe it's better to leave it here

HAFSAH. Hang on, leave it where? Why?

BILAL. You see it better than me
whatever I'm looking for, it's not *in* a language

HAFSAH. So where is it?

BILAL. I know enough to be content now, maybe not the
shaa'ir[20] I wanted to be but, understand my nani don't I?
I can leave it there

HAFSAH. Did you see your nani when you were home?

BILAL. Yeah, there's actually something I need to ask you
about that

HAFSAH. Oh god, what now?

BILAL. I've been wondering what you'd feel about Brum
Have you ever thought about living there?

HAFSAH. In Brum?
Why? You said you'd never want to live back there?

BILAL. I didn't tell you cos I wanted to tell you in person but
when I went home last week
things kicked off again with Danyaal, bad

Mum told me he'd come round a few days before I got home
asked if he could stay the night cos his place weren't safe

---

20. Poet.

She was scared so she said no and then
Hafs, Mum never cries but she
she just started crying in front of me in the kitchen

She said Danyaal

HAFSAH. **He goes quiet, rigid**
he's looking deep down into his tea

BILAL. Her whole cheek was purple Hafs

HAFSAH. Oh my god

BILAL. She's got no one – no husband, no one who can –
I can't abandon her Hafs

HAFSAH. You won't, you're not like them – not like your dad
or Danyaal

BILAL. This is why I'm nervous though Hafs

HAFSAH. Why?

BILAL. Would you consider us living at Mum's?
I know it's a big ask but
just so she's got someone

It'll mean we're not throwing money away
and I can help with the mortgage that way till –
dunno, what d'ya think?

Pause.

HAFSAH. But I thought we talked about this already
we agreed you're gonna meet my mum next month, then I'll
meet yours
and you said after I get my grade back we'll do a small
nikkah
I'll move in with you and apply for Islamic studies stuff till
you graduate and then we'll figure it out

What's –
you've said yourself so many times you don't want to be near
Danyaal or that /

BILAL. / I know I know but /

HAFSAH. / No listen, how would it help if you were there when
    Danyaal hit her?

BILAL. See that's the point, it wouldn't even get to that
    he wouldn't hit her if I was there

HAFSAH. Yeah cos he'd hit *you*

BILAL. Good, I'd finally be of some use

HAFSAH. You think that's *useful*?
    Has your mum ever actually *asked* you to do this?

    You haven't been home in years
    you went off to Kashmir, London, did your own thing
    Why is it suddenly like *you* need to be her guardian?

BILAL. No you're right – I *did* go off on my own flipping
    journey – this that, Pahari
    but that's *why* I've gotta step up now
    not just be the frigging, what everyone else has been

    I gotta be the man Hafs

HAFSAH. 'The man'?
    Are you joking? What is that?

    You think you can protect your mum, pay off her mortgage
    and *also* do your own thing with me?
    I have a right to my own –
    you don't even have a job Bilal

BILAL. And you said you were flipping alright with that!

HAFSAH. I *am* alright with that, but if you're meant to be 'the
    man' –

BILAL. What choice do I have?
    I can't abandon her

HAFSAH. Where was all this last month?
    You expect me to get on *your* rollercoaster
    but I'm on my own rollercoaster, Bilal, we all are –
    everyone's on one

    I'm not saying get on *mine*, but we *both* have to get on a third
    one

That's the whole point
We have to choose to step off our ones and step onto one
that's both of ours

But you can't see past your own rollercoaster

BILAL. I didn't ask to be on a flipping rollercoaster
not everyone can just step off Hafs
There's other people on this thing – who need me

HAFSAH. What about me?

You promised me Bilal
we had a plan
we had a whole –
I even told my sisters

HAFSAH *holds back tears.*

BILAL. Is moving in with my mum that bad?

HAFSAH. It's not about your mum, Bilal! I don't care where
I live!

It's that you want me to just slot into YOUR life
YOU don't want to be alone
YOU don't want to abandon your mum
YOU want to be a man
What about me?

You don't think I had my own plans? Dreams? Hopes?
I DO
I *have*
You were not a part of those, Bilal

But even then
I got ready to get off my rollercoaster

Got off and stood right here
I'm literally standing here
willing to choose a third way WITH YOU

But you're not choosing me back

Why won't you choose me back?

Eleven Months (October)

Russell Square.

BILAL. **We're sitting on a park bench in Russell Square**
   the **park bench**
   The one we've sat on a hundred times

   Both know why we're here
   sitting side by side means you don't have to look in each other's eyes
   you can be more honest that way, she told me that once

   We've spoke about everything, everything except the thing we have to say

   Her results come back tomorrow, the novella's finished
   she's got an agent, contract's signed for publication
   she hasn't got a reason to stay here any more

   But I can't say it
   She's always been braver than me

HAFSAH. **I didn't tell Mythri about this, she wouldn't have let me come**
   but she was proud of me for what I said
   though she had to have her little *I told you so* **moment of course**

   Hani said he's an f-boy and she always saw this coming
   despite *her* **being the one who told me to consider him in the first place**

   But they're both right
   he's selfish, yes, *but* **maybe in another world he –**
   maybe in a world where he had different, contexts, choices, I dunno

   I just wanted to give you this

   BILAL *reads the title.*

BILAL. *Deliverance from Error and Beginning of Guidance* by
   Al Ghazali

   He nods taking it in.

HAFSAH. I thought it'd be... helpful,
there'll be a reason this all happened, yeah?
Allahu alim[21] but there'll be good in it

BILAL. **I feel my face trembling
can't gulp**

HAFSAH. I had my first theology class today
we're just like fire – can't choose to be hot or cold
just 'kun fa ya kun' – be and it is – it's all just whatever Allah
wants

She chuckles dryly.

I just... really wish people told you that two people loving
each other is not enough

Long pause.

BILAL. You saying you love me?

HAFSAH *doesn't respond.*

**Her sadness is big but she can smile past it
Me though, I'm drowning**

HAFSAH. If it was meant to be, it wouldn't be this hard, would
it?

We're just choosing to accept Allah's plan for us
and that's right, right?

Pause.

What was it you said?
that story which can't be brought to a natural end?
It's better to leave it...

BILAL. **I wonder if this is a beautiful turning point or not
but I look at her sitting next to me
turquoise-blue hijab, eyes so gentle
looking at me in that way that nobody else does
course it is**

Beat.

---

21. God is the All-knowing/God knows.

HAFSAH. Just remember there'll be someone out there who can be what you need and someone who can be what I need / and

BILAL. / Don't –

HAFSAH. **He can barely speak and I don't ask him to**
I thought this would feel worse but somehow I'm stoic
Somehow I'm wiser than myself

BILAL. **We get up from the bench and start walking**

HAFSAH. **The trees witness like a funeral procession despite**
the sky being a beautiful blue

BILAL. Will you look me up?
Not now I mean – in the akhirah[22]

Ask for me, yeah? Maybe we can have another chance there

HAFSAH. I don't think that's how it works Bilal

BILAL. Will ya at least try?

HAFSAH. Why don't you ask for *me*?

BILAL. I will have been, that's why you gotta ask
So the angels can say
'Achhaaa, you mean the guy whose been asking about you
for millennia?'

HAFSAH. It's gonna take me millenia to remember you?

BILAL. Dunno, just think I'll leave the dunya before ya

HAFSAH. Don't say that

BILAL. **We reach her bike and she climbs on in the way I've**
seen her do a million times

HAFSAH. **He passes me my helmet in the way he's done**
a million times

BILAL. Ride safe yeah?

HAFSAH. Always do

My voice catches in my throat for a second but I have to
look him in the eye

You take care of yourself, okay?

---

22. Afterlife.

BILAL. **Both our eyes are wet**
funny to think that in all this time I never got to hold her

HAFSAH. May Allah be with you always, Bilal

And don't – don't say goodbye this time

I start pedalling, but after a second, he calls my name

BILAL. Hafs?

HAFSAH. I turn back for the last time

BILAL. See you in the akhirah, yeah?

End.

A Nick Hern Book

Peanut Butter & Blueberries first published in Great Britain as a paperback original in 2024 by Nick Hern Books Limited, The Glasshouse, 49a Goldhawk Road, London, W12 8QP in association with Kiln Theatre, London

Peanut Butter & Blueberries copyright © 2024 Suhaiymah Manzoor-Khan

Suhaiymah Manzoor-Khan has asserted her right to be identified as the author of this work

Cover photography by Michael Wharley

Designed and typeset by Nick Hern Books, London
Printed in Great Britain by Mimeo Ltd, Huntingdon, Cambridgeshire PE29 6XX

A CIP catalogue record for this book is available from the British Library

ISBN 978 1 83904 348 2

www.nickhernbooks.co.uk/environmental-policy

www.nickhernbooks.co.uk

facebook.com/nickhernbooks

twitter.com/nickhernbooks